FESTIVALS
AND CELEBRATIONS

Cover: miniature circus made by George Berger.
Front endpaper: view of the River Seine from the Pont-Neuf by an anonymous seventeenth-century French artist. (Carnavalet Museum, Paris)
Back endpaper: the carnival at Nice.

INTERNATIONAL LIBRARY

ROLAND AUGUET

FESTIVALS
AND CELEBRATIONS

COLLINS · PUBLISHERS   FRANKLIN WATTS, INC.

London · Glasgow   *New York*

CONTENTS

INTRODUCTION

From the beginning of recorded history people have arranged their lives as best they could within the framework imposed on them. Psychologists have not yet proved it, but it seems quite likely that there is a deep-felt need in human beings to celebrate, to break the monotonous routine of ordinary day-to-day existence.

The purpose of this book is to examine some of the highlights of man's past entertainments—the most significant festivals and spectacles of past times—and to trace their evolution to our own day. We shall also try to guess what the future holds to amuse us.

Before we pick up the thread of our narrative it may be worth asking if all celebrations are the same. After all, the person who attends a circus sits silent and motionless, so entranced that he hardly dares to look at his programme for fear of missing a single moment of the actual performance. He is an observer. What does he have in common with the wild, uncontrolled individual whirling madly along in a carnival procession? The latter is a participant.

It is a fact that the most violent, unrestrained feasting took place in brief, strikingly dramatic outbursts during periods of history when people were most heavily fettered by restraints of work or by the state. In ancient Rome, to pick the most obvious example, the huge masses of unemployed people were kept in a state of satisfactory political docility through an inspired programme of bread and circuses—the basic drive for food was satisfied and the unemployed occupied their time sitting as spectators in the amphitheatre. Leisure in Rome was thus a well-designed political weapon that became a way of life.

The disintegration of the Roman Empire left a void that was ultimately filled by the Church with its constraints on every aspect of man's terrestrial existence and the feudal economy that depended on the unremitting daily labour of all but the wealthiest members of society. The monotony of labour and saintliness was broken periodically by festivals that mixed paganism and Christianity in proportions that are most notable for their boundless joy and licence.

The rebuilding of the cities of Europe towards the end of the Middle Ages changed not only the face of the continent but also created a new world of freedom in which it was possible to experiment with varieties of diversion.

Cities became great centres of diversion. For some people simply to walk down the streets was an adventure, but even more important the cities became trend-setters, determining the patterns for the pleasures

Opposite: evening show.

Opposite: the carnival at Nice.

that would be enjoyed by entire populations. The coming of the Industrial Revolution enhanced this role of the cities and speeded the development of new refinements on themes developed in the oldest of man's celebrations.

Modern man, torn between the competitive allures of theatre, cinema, television, radio, racetrack, circus, football game, and a cycle of festive holidays, suffers from an embarrassment of riches that gives lie to the efforts of all the critics who bemoan the death of spontaneity and gaiety. It is undeniable that the shape of celebrations has changed, but that is precisely what has happened in every era up to our own.

Interneige 65.

A gladiator in the attack position. His right arm and left leg, which are more exposed than the rest of his body, are protected by strips of leather and metal. The helmet protects his head; to strike it was the equivalent of our "hitting below the belt" in boxing. The aim of the contest was to strike your opponent's body. (Municipal Museum, Mâcon)

CHAPTER 1

THE ROMAN GAMES

The Roman Games are renowned for their cruel bloodthirstiness. A whole society gloated over a man's death, which served as the instrument for collective pleasure. It is true that similar episodes have occurred in other societies and other periods of time. For instance, the people of the Middle Ages enjoyed attending spectacular executions, and the French Revolution had its *tricoteuses*, who knitted busily away at the foot of the guillotine, as people lost their heads. But these diversions were of a transitory nature. They never became, as in Rome, a permanent and institutionalized feature of the society.

The games were, above all, popular entertainments in the true sense of the word, watched by virtually the entire population. Moreover, they took place nearly every day.

No other society has ever indulged in such displays, not even modern Western society, which offers so much leisure to its citizens. In Rome, daily life was regulated by entertainment, not by work.

Entertainment and politics

In the first century BC, when the inefficiency and corruption of the republic provided an ideal breeding ground for ambitious men who sought personal power, the shows became a vital instrument of publicity and electoral propaganda. The politicians and generals (in Rome they were very often one and the same) provided splendid games in order to gain the popularity of the people and thus to make sure of their vote in the elections. No politician could afford to be stingy in this matter. Julius Caesar made good political capital out of the games. From the start of his career, he strove to provide memorable games for the citizens of Rome: 365 pairs of gladiators; silver armour; banquets; enormous elephant combats. The Roman people never forgot them—and Caesar became tribune of the people and dictator.

Eventually, the games became more important to the Romans than their daily bread. They were a luxury in their humdrum life. And they expected a high standard of performance. The emperors vied with each other to satisfy these demands. Some of them even took part in the chariot races or gladiatorial contests; others, in their efforts to ingratiate themselves with the spectators, behaved and spoke in the manner of the common people when they were in the amphitheatre. All of them, without exception, even those disgusted by the cruelties displayed in the arena, went to enormous trouble to organize the games.

The old country festivals of pre-

Julius Caesar. He began his political career by providing magnificent games. (Barracco Museum, Rome)

A gladiator's mask made from a sheet of copper. (Fenaille Museum, Rodez)

imperial Rome could not survive in the face of such magnificent displays. There were a large number of these picturesque, simple festivities, which carried on the oldest traditions of the land. The participants hunted the hare and goat in their neighbourhoods; they attached torches to the tails of foxes; they drank like fish; and they committed every kind of extravagance. But these pursuits became old-fashioned, gradually withered away and died out, making way for the new entertainment industry of the arena. In fact, it is scarcely an exaggeration to say that Rome invented show business.

The gladiators

Originally, gladiatorial combats were a "civilized" form of human sacrifice, with which the Romans hoped to ensure the immortality of their ancestors, in whose honour they were performed. Instead of killing a victim, prisoners of war were picked to fight each other to the death in front of the tomb of the departed. The earliest combats that we know about still preserved the appearance of a religious ceremony.

Under imperial rule, however, because of their political and public-relations importance, these combats developed into spectacular shows devoid of religious content. They were announced beforehand on inscribed placards placed near roadsides or on buildings. The day before the show, which sometimes lasted for more than a week, Rome teemed with milling countryfolk who had come into the city from the outlying regions. They camped right in the middle of the streets and there was such a crowd that people were reported to have suffocated and died in the crush.

To accommodate the huge number of spectators, a meticulous organization was set up. The vast amphitheatre called the Colosseum, which was begun during the reign of Vespasian in the first century AD, could seat five thousand spectators, but they were not allowed to push in wherever they chose. A strict system was devised whereby every Roman citizen sat in a specific section according to his social position. The higher the seats in the amphitheatre, the poorer the spectators. At the very top was the gallery, packed with the lowest classes—the slaves and foreigners who could not support themselves. Their seats reflected their status as the outcasts of Roman society. On the podium far below, where the emperor had his box, sat the members of the senate. Thus the seating arrangements in the Colosseum constituted a living incarnation of the city and its order. The Romans themselves were conscious of the fact that these shows brought out a strong feeling of unity among the diverse spectators—one might even call it a sense of communion.

The trident and the net

Sometimes what amounted to organized killings did take place in Rome. These events were usually carried out in the morning at a time when most of the people were at work and the amphitheatre was half empty. The real gladiatorial combats, however, had nothing to do with this kind of butchery. They were based on a precise science of swordsmanship. There were different categories of gladiators, each using its own special weapons and techniques. A strict code of rules governed the matching of one type of gladiator against another. It took into careful account their special characteristics, so that it was a reasonably fair fight. For example, a gladiator equipped with a strong system of defence—

shield and armour protecting his legs and arms, but fighting with the short sword—would be confronted by an adversary with practically no protective armour. The vulnerability of the latter, however, would be off-set by his use of particularly danger-ous and usually very long weapons. These enabled him to keep his op-ponent at a distance. Thus, not only two men but also two different techniques were in competition. Each type of gladiator had his own special tricks, his dangerous thrusts and his weak spots. The Thracian, for example, was famous for the low, skimming movement of his curved sword with which he struck a side-ways blow. The audience was well versed in all these subtleties and most critical of the quality of the combat. They made no allowance for inexperience or weakness; when they saw signs of either they whistled their disapproval and, at the end of the combat, would demand the death of the defeated gladiator. If the emperor turned his thumbs down as a sign that he shared the popular sentiment, the defeated gladiator was executed.

Two bronzes from the Rolin Museum in Autin. Above: a side attack, considered especially dangerous. Below: the metal plate attached to the gladiator's left shoulder protects him from side attacks.

One type of combat was especially popular because of its subtle and spectacular character. This was the gladiatorial combat between the *retiarus*, armed with a net, a trident, and sometimes a dagger, and the *secutor*, who was equipped with a sword and heavy shield. The *retiarus* matched his mobility against the strength and impact of the *secutor*. The *retiarus*, without a helmet or even leg armour to protect him, had at all costs to avoid a close en-counter in which he would almost certainly be beaten. He had to keep his opponent at a distance. Every time the *secutor* tried to close in on him, he would retreat. The combat thus developed into a series of short passes and withdrawals, performed

to the rhythm of music played by an orchestra. The *retiarus* would hurl his net forward, hoping to envelop his adversary and throw him to the ground. He was not always successful. His opponent staved off the net with his shield and charged. The *retiarus* had no time to draw back his net, so he had to change his method of attack. He seized his trident, which he normally carried in the left hand, with both hands and charged, trying to wound the *secutor* above or below the shield—this tactic is illustrated in the mosaic on the right. If he was unfortunate enough to get his trident stuck or to drop it, he knew he was in danger of losing his life. Now he had nothing but a small dagger with which to defend himself against far more powerful weapons.

Quite often two gladiators, as they came into close contact, would roll on to the ground. On Roman oil lamps they are depicted struggling on the sand in a clinch, each man fighting with just a sword. If his opponent gave him the opportunity, the defeated gladiator would raise his thumb to ask for mercy. It was then up to the emperor and the public to decide whether he should be spared. If he was spared and defeated a second time, however, he was given no mercy.

For all their excitement, after a while these combats began to pall on the audiences who had seen thousands of them. New ideas were needed to keep the crowd satisfied. The almost routine nature of the games, after they had been held nearly every day for years, inevitably led to a search for more picturesque and sensational novelties. The organizers borrowed and adapted some of the more curious techniques of fighting that were practised by their subjugated peoples. They arranged combats between dwarfs

A contest between a retiarus *and a* secutor. *In the middle is their trainer who acts as referee. (Mosaic from the Villa of Nennig, Saarbrücken, Staatliches Konservatoramt)*

There was a continual search for new amusements to entertain the blasé public. This contest involves a whip and a cudgel. (Mosaic from the Villa of Nennig)

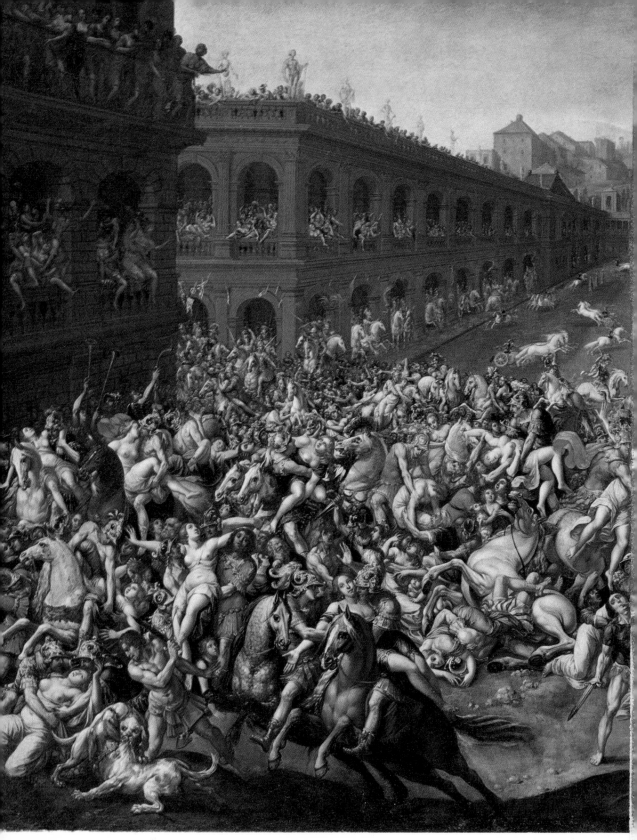

The Rape of the Sabines *by Deruet.*
Legend has it that this famous episode
in Roman history took place while the
warriors were absorbed in watching the
games. (Alte Pinakothek, Munich)

A gladiator with a movable mask. (Lapidary Museum, Arles)

and women, between whole troops of gladiators, and even between blind men, or, to be more precise, gladiators whose heads were covered by helmets without visors, so that the combat took on the appearance of a tragicomedy. There were even combats in which the defeated man was not allowed to raise his thumb and ask for mercy. He had no choice but to accept death on the spot. Emperor Augustus (27 BC– AD 14) put a stop to these cruel combats, but after his death, his interdiction was overlooked.

It seems monstrous to us that the writers, philosophers, and elite of Roman society should have protested so little against such extreme acts of cruelty. On reflection, however, it is obvious that they were not in a position to do so. As already mentioned, these entertainments played a vital role in the political and social system of Rome. To have criticized the games, therefore, would have meant questioning the whole structure of Roman civilization, including slavery—the foundation of ancient societies. For the gladiators were, to all intents and purposes, slaves, and the Romans believed that a slave was not a human being and that they could do what they liked to him.

Wild animal hunts

Another typical Roman entertainment, which actually originated in Carthage, was the wild animal hunt or combat. There were many variations. Sometimes the animals were forced to fight each other. All kinds of subterfuges were used in order to incite the animals. For example, a bull and a panther were chained together, so that the two animals, enraged by the harness, tore each other to pieces in a fight in which neither was the victor. At other times

condemned men were thrown to the wild beasts without any weapons with which to defend themselves. In such cases, the entertainment consisted solely of contemplating death. The Romans themselves found this type of animal hunt distasteful and degrading. Indeed, contrary to what some novels and films would have us believe, this form of sport was not very popular. The men who were put to death in this way (to be thrown to the wild beasts in the arena was legally an extension of the death penalty) were, in the first place, slaves condemned for some very serious offence, or prisoners of war who were considered highly dangerous. Later on, it was Christians, who did not qualify as Roman citizens, who were thrown to the wild animals.

The authentic wild animal hunt, as far as the public was concerned, was a combat between wild beasts and specially trained men who had adopted the hunting techniques of African and Asian peoples. They would pierce the panther with a javelin, attack the bear with a hunting spear· and, on occasions, they would confront the bull with just their bare hands. These combats were not always individual ones. Sometimes about twenty or more lions were released into the arena matched against a small troop of these specialists who were called bestiaries, or *venatores*.

Before the Colosseum was built, the presentation of wild animal hunts, even when unaccompanied by the refinements of a complicated stage direction, created serious problems. They took place in the Circus Maximus where few precautions were taken to safeguard the lives of the spectators. On one occasion the show nearly turned to disaster. About twenty elephants were fighting the Getulians, a north

The fight of the gladiators. On the left is the orchestra, following the tempo of the struggle. (Zliten Mosaic, Tripoli Museum)

A bestiary. (Mosaic from the Villa of Nennig)

African people who were used to this type of combat. They had perfected very effective techniques, using javelins. They would paralyse the elephant by piercing its foot, or they would kill it with a single blow by aiming their javelins at the eye and piercing the brain. The Romans were full of admiration for the amazing skill of the Getulians. On that particular occasion, however, the herd of elephants became disturbed, either by wounding or fear, and suddenly charged at the iron railings that served as the barrier separating the audience from the arena. Wild panic spread through the rows of spectators. Fortunately, thanks to the prompt action of the Getulians, the Romans escaped with nothing more than a bad fright. The railings withstood the attack long enough to prevent a catastrophe.

The wild animal trade

Accidents such as these were insignificant problems compared to the difficulty involved in the capture and transportation to Rome of the rare and dangerous animals that were needed for the entertainments. As many as five thousand animals might be killed in a single event.

First a stock of animals was needed. It was provided, in part, by the imperial menageries, which were organized to receive and maintain many thousands of animals. They were fed by means of an elaborate network of supply that extended throughout the empire. The sole

The Consul Aerobindus throws the white cloth, which was the starting signal for the races in the Byzance Hippodrome. (Ivory plaque in the Cluny Museum, Paris)

task of certain units of the Roman legions stationed in such provinces as Nubia, Mesopotamia, and north Africa was to capture wild animals. The animals were then put into crates and taken to the Italian peninsula by ship. The slowness of this form of transport, of course, led to the death of many animals.

Most of the wild beasts were brought from Africa where the Romans organized huge safaris with the help of the Africans, who had perfected a wide range of techniques for capturing the animals. They encircled them and then, with the aid of lighted torches, herded the animals towards enclosures or traps they had prepared beforehand. It was not exactly a peaceful form of sport and the mosaics that remain often depict dramatic scenes where a man, caught unawares by the sudden attack of a wild beast, lost his life through a careless blunder or a few seconds' lack of concentration.

The provision of wild beasts for the amphitheatre created considerable economic activity, as did, of course, the other branches of entertainment in Rome. A number of private individuals thereby made their fortune, and some African ports owed their prosperity to it.

Above: a disarmed bestiary, who has been baiting a bear, takes refuge in a vat with a false bottom. (Engraved marble plaque, Narbonne Museum). Below: leading wild animals to the ships which will transport them to Rome. (Mosaic, Pizza Armerina, Sicily)

The chariot races

Nowadays, horse racing has become a form of gambling rather than an entertainment, but this was not the case in ancient Rome. Although private bets were exchanged between individuals, it was only to enhance the excitement of the spectacle.

Chariot racing was enormously popular. On the day when it took place, the city was deserted. Matters came to such a pass during the reign of Augustus that they had to post soldiers on special duty throughout the city to prevent

thieves from robbing the temptingly empty houses. All the Romans, as well as large numbers of provincials —a crowd of 200,000 to 250,000 people—would pack the Circus Maximus. The tiered rows of seats were packed with a colourful, disorderly array of people, pushing and shoving, shouting to each other, swearing at one another. Sometimes they even came to blows over their seats or in defence of their particular "colour."

The competitors, in fact, belonged to four different factions, or stables: the Whites, the Blues, the Reds, and the Greens. Each of the groups had its own fervent supporters among the spectators. The colours were worn by the charioteers and displayed on the harnesses of the horses, so that they could be seen clearly as the chariots completed the seven laps of the race round the central *spina*—"backbone"—of the track. *Ben Hur* and other films have shown

us what the chariot race was like. It demanded the utmost skill and courage on the part of the drivers. The whole art of the race lay in the drivers' ability to steer the chariots successfully round the turning posts at each end of the track. It was vital not to be pushed to the outside. At the same time, if the charioteers hugged the turning post too closely, they ran the risk of knocking into it. They also had to be on the lookout for other charioteers who might run into them, either accidentally or deliberately. For, just as in modern horse racing, every competitor was out to obstruct or hem in his rivals. Sometimes they took enormous risks to do so. A charioteer might even try to eliminate his rival by crashing into his chariot. The fragile body of the chariot would shatter under the impact, causing the horses to collapse to the ground. The charioteer avoided being dragged along the ground by taking his

dagger and quickly severing the reins that were fixed round his waist and which attached him to his team of horses.

The passion of the public for these races has been criticized by some Roman writers. It is true that at times it degenerated into absurdity. Fanatics committed suicide on the tombs of charioteers; horses were allowed the run of the palace, or were fed on raisins out of feeding-troughs made of precious metals. It was not just a question of aristocratic fads. The common people worshipped the charioteers, following them through the streets as if they were gods. They seemed to think of nothing but the races all day long and were certainly fanatics of the sport. Yet, it should be remembered that this fanaticism had its roots in the "leisure" forced on people by unemployment, and the lack of political consciousness of the masses.

An elephant is coaxed on board for the voyage to Rome. This was a delicate operation owing to the terror of the huge animal. (Mosaic, Piazza Armerina, Sicily)

Opposite above: reconstruction of the Circus in Rome. This was where chariot races were held. It had also been the scene of wild animal hunts which were later held in the Colosseum. (Anonymous engraving, circa 1600)

Pariahs and idols

Every big show has its stars. Rome was no exception. There was Hermes, the unbeatable gladiator; Carphorus, the animal trainer, whose praises were sung by the poets; Scorpus, the charioteer who had two thousand victories to his credit. The public clamoured and shouted for them at the top of their voices. Women admired them. Emperors showered them with gold.

It seems, therefore, that the men who faced such perils in the arena were at least rewarded with glory and riches. This was true up to a point for the successful ones, but even they did not have the right to determine their own lives, or even to give up their careers if they wished. They were slaves, forced to submit to the will of their masters and the whims of the public.

In any case, not many of them achieved stardom. The vast majority led a hard life with few compensations. What kind of a man became a gladiator? Very often he was a slave, in other words a pariah, sold by his master to the director of a troop of gladiators because he had a strong physique or, perhaps, to punish him for some stupid action, which happened quite frequently. The young man might be eighteen years old when he first came to the barracks. The training began by "breaking him in." He was whipped —a symbolic gesture to remind him that he owed absolute obedience to his masters. Next, he was sent to the training school. He was taught all the tricks of the trade by a specialist. He exercised on "the pole" to make his body supple. He practised fighting with a wooden sword and then with a sword heavier than the normal ones, so that he got used to making a greater effort than he would require in a real gladiatorial combat. What did he get in exchange for all this? A roof over his head (the barracks), food, and a small bonus on enlistment.

At last the time came for the gladiator's first combats in the arena. They were difficult days, for the public took little interest in beginners and were quick to condemn them when they were beaten. Some of the gladiators died very young. But what of the gladiators who survived the ordeal of these early combats? After several years, when a gladiator had completed his period of service, he had the right to leave the barracks. More often than not, he re-enlisted. He might not have saved up enough money to change to another way of life. And, besides, he was sure to be offered better conditions if he re-enlisted. His life was valued a little more highly now. Usually he could not resist the temptation, even though he knew that death lay in wait for him.

But one must remember that the Romans were a nation of warriors; death was not important to them. In their eyes, it was an honour for a slave to face death in the amphitheatre. They believed that in so doing, he showed himself to be the equal of a free man and of a soldier.

The end of the games

It is often claimed that the Roman Games were brought to an end by Christianity. This is not so. New ideas, however powerful, could not destroy a custom that, economically and politically, had played such a vital role in Roman life for centuries.

The games actually died out through lack of funds. As the empire's economy crumbled, emperors were forced to give away to private individuals their wild animals because they could no longer afford their upkeep.

Opposite below: a chariot race. (Bas-relief, British Museum, London)

CIRCI ET QVINQVE LVDICRORVM CIRCENSIVM EX PRISCIS MONVMENTIS GRAPHICA DEFORMATIO ONVPHRII PANVINII

CIRCVS

Pag. 62.

T.337.

... ses sont de grant maniere   L vns auoit ... a ...
... vns ont te deuant darriere   C ... sus aissees ce ste naches
... lui et ... seur ...   E ... ...

CHAPTER 2

THE FEAST OF FOOLS

The theatre cannot exist unless there are spectators, and in the first centuries of the Middle Ages there were none, for obvious reasons. Towns were few and far between, money a rarity, and most of the population, dispersed over the vast feudal estates, lived in a closed economy. The Roman amphitheatres, scattered over Gaul and the Rhineland, where musical shows —combining the Roman style with local folklore—had once been performed, had fallen into disuse.

Mystery plays

It was not until the thirteenth century that an original form of popular entertainment emerged: the mystery plays. These mysteries re-enacted the most moving episodes in the Holy Scriptures and, in particular, the Passion of Christ. Originally, they were performed inside churches with priests as actors, but it was not long before they were performed outside, in front of the church. The performance usually went on for several days, for the texts of these early mystery plays were weighed down by interminable theological discussions, which are usually cut out of modern adaptations. Sometimes the plays were tens of thousands of verses long, as for example, the fourteenth-century *Passion of Arnoul Gréban*, which

had 34,574 verses. The plays were staged in elaborate productions, as is shown in the documents reproduced here. All the scenes of action were represented at the same time on the stage, including Heaven and Hell, which was filled with crowds of picturesque devils. Gradually, more and more profane scenes were added to the mysteries to heighten the dramatic effect.

As time passed, the mysteries gradually changed into a profane form of entertainment that the crowd came to see for relaxation and amusement. Yet, originally, their aim had been to create an imagery, drawn from the Holy Scriptures, which would provide spiritual nourishment for the ignorant masses. They had also served as useful propaganda by putting the fear of God into the spectators. Hell played a prominent role in these plays with its shrieks of despair, its devils spitting fire, and the laments of the damned.

In short, the mystery plays were one of the many manifestations of an age obsessed by salvation.

Organized sacrilege

It was during this same period of history, with all its burning piety, that a parody of religion emerged in the shape of grotesque ceremonies, performed with a wild fantasy and

Opposite: Charivari, a noisy burlesque procession similar to those which took place during the Feast of Fools. (Miniature by Roman de Fauvel, Bibliothèque Nationale, Paris)

Opposite above:
performance of a
mystery play. A
detail from the
Miracle of Theophilus.
(Tympanum in Notre
Dame Cathedral,
Paris)

violence unimaginable in any other epoch. The best known is the Feast of Fools, which took place between Christmas and Twelfth Night in many parts of Europe. We know quite a lot about this feast from contemporary writings:

The Feast of Fools showed us clerics and priests, masked and wearing women's clothes. They danced in the church, sang lewd songs, played dice and devoured meat on the altar where Mass was celebrated; meanwhile, others with blasphemous derision, filled the church with a sickening odour by burning pieces of old leather in the censers. In the midst of these saturnalia, were wretched creatures decked out as bishops, wearing a mitre and holding the cross in the hand. They would bestow mock blessings on the crowd who would roar with delight. In Antibes, the lay brothers of a certain monastery, on the day of this horrible feast, dressed themselves up in priests' clothing all torn, tattered or worn inside out, and made their way to the chancel in this outfit. There they held a travesty of a service during which all the brothers, their faces decorated with spectacles, whose lenses were replaced by pieces of orange peel, intoned prayers before a book held upside down, while writhing and twisting their bodies in the most obscene manner.

These feasts were doubly sacrilegious. First, because they took place within churches, the people feasting and carousing while the scene just described was going on. Second, because although brotherhoods like the Confrérie de la Mère Folle at Dijon took part in the organization of these feasts, the actors were very often priests.

They started off by electing a bishop, who was enthroned with ridiculous ceremonies. After having decked him out in robes of green and yellow, they solemnly handed him the bishop's wand of office, mitre and cross. Then, escorted by the

crowd, and preceded by a torchlight and candlelight procession, the "bishop" made his way to the church where he celebrated Mass, decked out in these absurd clothes.

Meanwhile, his companions, masked, smeared with must and dressed up as madmen, monstrous beasts, prostitutes or mountebanks, danced the round in the middle of the church; they ran and jumped wildly through the church, their bodies writhing in strange contortions and screaming out blasphemies at the top of their voices, which were greeted with laughter by all those present. . . . Later on, the actors rode through the town in dung-carts filled with garbage, which they threw at the passersby. The priests took off their cassocks and danced in the streets. Very often the laymen and priests mingled together, exchanging clothing with each other.

A concert of cats

These feasts were nothing out of the ordinary; they did not serve as an emotional outlet for eccentric sects. It seems they were called the Feast of the Drunken Deacons in some places, not because it was only deacons who took part in them but because the deacons got drunk during the festivities. There were many variations, all mixed up with each other, and it would take a whole book to describe them properly.

One particular variation was very popular during the Middle Ages, perhaps because of its grotesque and comic elements. This was the Donkey's Festival. The following is a description of one of the many versions of this ceremony, which took place at Beauvais:

A very beautiful girl was selected and, carrying a child in her arms, was placed on a donkey wearing a cope. The procession, led by the crowd and the

Opposite below: this
canvas, scenery for
mystery plays, was
painted circa 1530.

cathedral clergy, proceeded to the church of Saint-Etienne, where they were received by the canons, bottle and glass in hand. The Mass began. The first psalm was sung, but was ended by the cry of "hee-haw." This joke was repeated at the end of the service when the priest intoned "hee-haw" three times, to which the congregation replied "*Deo gratis* hee-haw!"

A procession that took place in Brussels in 1549 bears some resemblance to these comic ceremonies. It is worth describing because of its originality. A large procession of carts, some led by a child dressed up as a wolf and walking by the side of the Archangel Gabriel, displayed the most extraordinary sights. On one of them, about twenty or more crates contained cats whose tails were attached with rope to the register of an organ. The organist was a man dressed up as a bear. On pressing the keys of the organ, he pulled the tails of the cats, who miaowed frantically. Bears, wolves, deer, and crowds of other animals danced to the sound of this strange music. The writer who described this ceremony remarks that the cats "never sang a note out of tune."

He who is mad is wise

What was the cause of these violent explosions? First, speaking in general terms, feasts are, in a sense, a reaction against the *moral* discipline imposed on us by society. This will become more obvious in the case of carnivals. As far as the Feast of Fools was concerned, this discipline—which today takes the form of moral and social prohibitions—found expression in the Middle Ages in religious taboos. Respect for these taboos was not just a question of salvation or damnation; it was quite simply a matter of life or death. In those days,

men were burned at the stake for trivial offences.

Thus, during festivities like the Feast of Fools, medieval people made a point of attacking the most sacred of these taboos: they feasted and caroused on the altar as if they were in a tavern; they scoffed at the holy books and the Mass with donkey's braying; they held the bishop's person up to ridicule; and they brazenly defied the sexual taboos with obscene songs and dances. Their derision knew no bounds—with one exception. They drew the line at the tabernacle. They were delighted to ridicule the representatives of God and His church, but not Christ Himself, or, in other words, the host.

That may sound surprising, but there is a profound need in man to deny the most serious beliefs and institutions by reducing them to the level of buffoonery. It is a characteristic of many societies. The feast is the negation of order. Society, unable to control the anarchy within it, has organized and channelled it into the feast. It has given it the appearance of an institution. The derision expressed in the festivities has no practical consequences, for it bears no relation to reality. The day after the Feast of Fools, the participants became good, pious Christians once again, without any regrets. They never dreamed of seriously questioning the structure of society. Medieval people thought of the feast as a digression, as a temporary madness. For us it seems more like a release of frustrations.

Yet it is a madness full of wisdom. The standard of the Confrérie de la Mère Folle at Dijon bears the words: "He who is mad is wise." The temporary negation of normal values still helps us to accept in our day-to-day life a social discipline whose absurdity and injustice grow unbearable at times. It remains to be seen how the medieval church, so authoritarian and critical, which did not even admit the concept of doubt, could accept being ridiculed in this way.

A topsy-turvy world

Here we turn to the social aspect of the Feast of Fools, perhaps the most interesting side of it. Not all the clergy took part in these festivities. It was the privilege of the lower clergy and common people who, in

this way, could take a symbolic revenge upon the higher clergy. A verse they sang during the feast is typical of their state of mind: "The good Lord has brought low the powerful, and raised up the humble." And a historian wrote: "The Feast

The Bal des Ardents *at the court of Charles VI. The participants are disguised as animals and the torches are used to set light to their costumes. (Froissart Chronicle, Bibliothèque Nationale, Paris)*

An example of one of the fantastic carriages used during the Feast of Fools.

of Fools, like the Saturnalia, was the temporary emancipation of the underlings. They celebrated their one-day rule by committing excesses as senseless as they were short-lived; the hierarchy was upturned and normal roles reversed by the enthronement of clerics, choir boys, deacons and humble priests." This reversal of social roles, epitomized by the comic ceremony of the bishop's enthronement, was also to be found in the Saturnalia, which took place in December of every year in ancient Rome. For several days, the slaves did not have to submit to any authority; sometimes they even had the right to give orders to their masters. The world had been turned upside down.

Not surprisingly, the ecclesiastical

authorities had little sympathy with the Feast of Fools. They mistrusted this satirical outburst against them. Although it was apparently nothing more than a temporary madness, a comic fantasy totally devoid of revolutionary content, they saw in it the seeds of unrest. Besides, these feasts served to revive pagan beliefs deep rooted in the people: they were rather like anti-mystery plays. For a long time the Church had no choice but to put up with them, because it was difficult to eradicate traditions that answered certain basic human needs, and of whose significance some of the clergy were aware. Finally the Church condemned them officially but none too effectually at the Council of Basle in 1431.

During the sixteenth century, in

In some towns, the Feast of Fools was organized by groups who had emblems. Some of them are shown here. The plates illustrate dissertations to be used at the Feast of Fools. (Opéra Library, Paris)

nitre   LE ROI   HENRY   CATHERINE de   7 8   D'ANJOU LE DUC D'ALENÇON ELISABETH d'Autriche 10 Charles de BOURBON MARGUERITE 12 Claude 13 14   MARIE 1559
bleau   duc de Guise Médicis Reine-mère 5   6 Henry d'Alsace 2 Claude 4   3 le roi 4 Roi de   11 Louis de Luxembourg   11 Claude de Lorraine

face of growing hostility, the Feast of Fools gradually died out. Nevertheless, it remained deep rooted in local custom. During the reign of Louis XIV, it still occurred from time to time in the south of France. According to the American writer Harvey Cox, the disappearance of the Feast of Fools marked a turning point in the history of our civilization. Let us say rather that it represented a profound change of attitude. The Feast of Fools embodied certain cultural values: imagination, fantasy and, most of all, a feeling for satire. These values have gradually been sacrificed by Western society in favour of efficiency, rationalism, and productivity. The disappearance , of the Feast of Fools coincided with the dawn of a new world.

At the time when the Feast of Fools was dying out, other kinds of shows were gaining popularity, in particular the commedia dell'arte *which spread throughout Europe. A performance at the court of Charles IX is shown here. (Bayeux Museum)*

33

CHAPTER 3

MOUNTEBANKS

Apart from brief, intense festivities such as the Feast of Fools and the pre-Lenten Carnival, which marked the high spots of the year, the most outstanding popular shows in pre-industrial society were provided by the mountebanks, or travelling showmen. Every day, in all the large cities of Europe, they were to be found on some busy corner entertaining the crowds. Later on, the circus took over the best of their shows, adapting them to modern tastes.

From the sixteenth century on, large numbers of these travelling showmen came to live in Venice. They settled in the Via San Marco, next to the San Marco Basilica. According to a contemporary traveller, it was a very busy thoroughfare, frequented each day by thousands of people. The mountebanks, who were known in Italian as *montambanci* because they delivered their pitch from a small bench or platform, would amuse the crowds with every kind of entertainment, accompanied by gay and noisy music. These shows were partly improvised theatre, performed by actors who sometimes joined the professional companies of the *commedia dell'arte*, and partly fairground acts. These performances were not put on for their own sake, but served as a form of publicity. At the end of the performance, the mountebanks would produce various articles from their chests and try to sell them to the public. They had a vast selection of goods: love songs, trinkets, ointments for healing wounds and burns, and all kinds of other medicines. Some of the medicines were supposed to possess magic properties, such as the elixir of life; others were merely picturesque, as for instance, an ointment for improving the memory, or spectacles for seeing in the dark.

The ballad singers

The mountebanks naturally chose the busiest parts of the town to carry on their hazardous profession. Their presence, which added considerably to the commotion in the streets, turned the place they had selected into a centre of popular life. The Pont-Neuf in Paris is a good example. This bridge, crossing the Seine from the Louvre to the Left Bank, was filled with a constant stream of noisy people from morning to night.

The whole place swarmed with activity. In the midst of the booksellers and secondhand dealers could be seen a motley collection of mountebanks: sellers of rat poison and of all sorts of medicine; chiropodists who removed corns; orthopedists who made wooden legs "to repair the violence of bombs";

Opposite: the Imprenuta Fair in Florence. (After Jacques Callot, Bargoin Museum, Clermont-Ferrand)

Commerce and the theatre combine — Italian jugglers and, at the far side of the stage, an "actor" displaying his wares. (Lacroix, Bibliothèque Nationale, Paris)

Opposite: view of the Pont-Neuf thoroughfare and showground. All along the bridge are the stalls of the booksellers, who sold songs and pamphlets called mazarinades. (Anonymous seventeenth-century French, Carnavalet Museum, Paris)

tooth-pullers; *tisane*-sellers who crossed the bridge calling out, "Freshly made tea! Freshly made tea!" To the noisy accompaniment of passing carriages, Brioché the puppeteer presented to the public his monkey dressed up in doublet and ruff.

In addition to these types of showmen, who were to be found in every town of Europe, the Pont-Neuf had its own special brand of strolling entertainers. First, there were the ballad singers who, in a few verses, mourned the death of a condemned man who had been hanged or broken on the wheel, or who sang about the misfortune of some poor wretch who had just been assassinated. Certain singers, it seems, when short of a subject, fell back on religious hymns. But that could not have happened very often. The Pont-Neuf had acquired such an evil reputation that the country-folk from the provinces were scared to venture there even during the day. People were assassinated without a second thought and, unless the victim was a well-known personality, no one took any notice of a corpse. It was merely thrown into the Seine with no further to-do. Hangings took place, too. The Royal Justice

erected the gallows there to impress the public by these executions "presented in tableaux," as an official document of the period put it. The common people, too, erected their own gallows, usually symbolic ones. One day, for instance, they displayed the corpse of a favourite who had been assassinated; later on, they even hung the effigy of Mazarin, the French statesman and Roman Catholic cardinal. The ballad singers were rarely short of inspiration.

Other singers went in for that most perilous of styles—political satire. At least they sang them until the mid-seventeenth century when Louis XIV established his auto-cratic rule, which frowned on any criticism, even in song. The singing satirists were not the only people to attack authority. At the time of the Fronde (1648–53), during which the nobility tried to stem the growth of the king's authority, it was on the Pont-Neuf that the booksellers set up their stalls. Their pamphlets and satirical broadsides criticizing the regime were so successful that they were finally forbidden to sell them.

The singers made use of any items of news that came their way. The moment some interesting event occurred in the court or in the country, they were quick to satirize it. They sang of duels and betrayals, of the defeats of generals and ministers; and their songs spread like wildfire through the city and became so well known that soon the singers were called quite simply the *Ponts-Neufs*. "Look out for the *Ponts-Neufs*!" cried the Great Condé to his officers as he was about to go into battle with his enemies. And Mazarin is said to have made the cynical remark, "Let them sing, so long as they pay." The government, however, mistrusted these songs in spite of their apparent good humour and gaiety.

The ointment from Peru

Imagine what it must have been like on the Pont-Neuf and similar places, where every type of mountebank was to be found clamouring for attention: conjurors who swallowed a bucket of clear water and then brought it up again in whatever colour was asked for by the audience; puppeteers with their marionettes and freaks, both real and fake, such as the huge, wooden, ventriloquists' figures that were made to speak in a thin, high voice; tightrope-walkers; and, of course, jugglers of every sort and size, such as the one who was reputed to have nailed eight watches to the ceiling with pistol shots, after having thrown them into the air.

The profession of mountebank also included all those who practised popular medicine. They were called surgeons, quacks, or charlatans, but they liked to be known by the rather pompous title of "Spagyrical Doctors." Among the marvels they sold were "an ointment from Peru, which makes the complexion as clear as a mirror" or "a quintessence from China which enlarges the eyes, pulls together the corners of the mouth, lengthens noses that are too small and reduces ones that are too big." Other doctors specialized in pulling teeth. In their sales talk, one and all used a mixture of exotic references and scholarly language, of buffoonery and Greek words— that must have profoundly impressed their audience, so avid for marvels.

The most amusing aspect is that the Faculty of Medicine at the university was very upset on more than one occasion by the competition offered by this noisy, unruly confraternity. Perhaps this was because the quacks were so quick to pick up the medical jargon of the day. On various occasions officials of the medical profession published very pompous pamphlets with such titles as, "The Frauds of the Charlatans Exposed," and even obtained permission from the authorities to apply sanctions against them, which were never used, however. The common people preferred these miracle-makers to the solemn doctors who inflicted more or less the same treatment on them, but without making them laugh. Besides, in those days there were few public centres for medical care, and these open-air clinics were needed.

Charlatanism and magic

Brioché was a happy man and, as the saying goes, happiness has no tale to tell. His marionette shows were always attended by large crowds, even when his rivals introduced more elaborate techniques in the Parisian theatres. Perhaps he owed this success to his jokes. Or maybe they came to see his monkey Fagotin, which was said to be as "stout as a paté from Amiens" and which he dressed up in a doublet with six basques flowing from it, in order to enliven the parade he put on before the show began.

But Brioché, weary of his Parisian success, wanted a change of audience. One fine day he arrived in a small town buried in the heart of Switzerland and set up his theatre there. The local people hurried along to see the show, for there was little entertainment in that part of the world. When they caught sight of the little figures of the marionettes speaking and laughing, a murmur of fear ran through the audience. The spectators were soon convinced that these tiny beings were creatures of the devil, that Brioché was travelling round the world accompanied by a troop of little devils, that he had a pact with Satan. They went off to find the magistrate, who threw the puppeteer into prison.

This anecdote shows the wide difference in outlook between cityfolk and country people and is only one example of many similar incidents that occurred at that time. Even as late as the seventeenth century, the inhabitants of remote villages believed that mountebanks and sorcerers were one and the same thing. A contemporary writer recalls that when the Italian actor Monferino found himself in a similar plight in a small village, the local council held a stormy meeting and expelled him from the village on the charge of practising magic. In the south of France during the same period, a mountebank, who had

Tumblers.
(Bibliothèque
Nationale, Paris)

invented a skeleton who played the guitar, was hanged and then burned along with his invention. Brioché was luckier. One of the captains of the guard explained everything to the magistrate who released the prisoner.

Tooth-pullers

The quack dentists were the most popular and colourful of all the mountebanks. They wore strings of teeth round their necks as a sign of their trade, and displayed a jumble of incredible relics in front of their booths, including such bizarre items as stuffed crocodiles. Their methods of extracting teeth were a traditional subject of humour. In spite of the powders they used with great ostentation to "anaesthetize" the patient, they usually resorted to cruder methods, if one is to believe the following description: "He had no trouble in drawing the tooth when it was loose; but when it was a tough one to budge, he made the patient kneel down and raised him from the ground as many as three times with the strength of a bull. So much for the lower jaw. When it came to the upper jaw, he might even resort to using a winch!"

Of course, they claimed this kind

of operation was painless. In order to convince their clients, the tooth-puller would give a demonstration. All he had to do was to make a deal with an accomplice, who would allow himself to be hacked around, while pretending to be most satisfied with the treatment. The best way of assuring a successful demonstration was to provide the accomplice with a few false teeth patched with red paint. If he did not take such a precaution, things could go wrong. This happened to Cormier, for instance, one of the stars of the Pont-Neuf. He made a deal with a half-starved poet called Sibus, promising to pay him ten sous in return for extracting two teeth "painlessly." So one fine morning, Cormier gathered a crowd around him and began to extol the miraculous ease of his operations. Suddenly a voice was raised in the crowd:

"I can't sleep at night nor during the day, any more than a lost soul can!" Cormier shouted back to the "unknown" speaker that he had better watch out. His teeth were clearly in a very bad condition and he might lose them all. The poor wretch approached. It was Sibus. Cormier, after examining his teeth, discovered a large number of decayed ones and began to operate as arranged. He had scarcely begun before the poet suddenly began to leap up and down, his body stiffened, and he let out such piercing shrieks that Cormier was forced to stop work several times. Immediately, Sibus, looking ghastly and trembling, his forehead bathed in sweat and his mouth full of blood, turned to the audience and exclaimed: "Ah! That was marvellous! It didn't hurt a bit!" Finally, Cormier had to be satisfied with drawing one tooth

Street farces were the most popular form of entertainment. (Anonymous seventeenth-century French, Carnavalet Museum, Paris)

41

One of the stars of the Saint-Laurent Fair, where the tumblers also gathered.

Gautier-Garguille (above) and Guillot-Gorju (below) were two celebrities of the popular show.

only. He refused to pay the poet the agreed sum of ten sous because he had not complied with the clauses of their contract.

Apart from Cormier, Big Thomas was one of the most celebrated tooth-pullers of the Pont-Neuf. Like so many of the mountebanks, he possessed a magnificent physique. According to a song that went the rounds after his death, his talents were not limited to the practice of dentistry:

"Liver and kidneys that he tended
Were by his remedies quite
    mended
And by a secret known to him,
For every sickness, for all ills
In human beings and in horses
He gave them both the same size
    pills."

This generosity showed itself in more spectacular ways, which seems to have contributed a good deal to his popularity. For instance, he would offer his services free of charge, especially on important occasions. A contemporary gazette solemnly announced that "Big Thomas, wishing to express his joy at the recovery of His Majesty, has pulled teeth free of charge for three days on the Pont-Neuf. He likewise visited prisons and hospitals and pulled teeth free there."

"To lie like a tooth-puller," goes the saying, and one day, in a burst of generosity, Big Thomas unwittingly confirmed the truth of it. He told people that he was going to invite them to a meal on the Pont-Neuf. The feast was to take place on the following Monday. Several days beforehand, he bought all the necessary food and drink. He even went so far as to have menus printed. For some unknown reason, however, the police lieutenant took fright at the prospect of this unusual celebration and forbade Big Thomas

to show himself on the Pont-Neuf on the Monday in question. When a large crowd congregated on the bridge that day not a crumb of food was to be seen. The Parisians, believing that Big Thomas had played a trick on them, besieged him in his home. Before he had time to explain, they had smashed his windows. His popularity, however, does not seem to have suffered too greatly from this unfortunate mishap.

Tabarin makes his fortune

This anecdote reveals the social importance acquired by the most popular mountebanks. They were the big popular stars if their day. Their fame had spread even to the royal court where they used to perform shows, and the king conferred titles on them. Thus, Brioché the puppeteer could boast of being "Puppeteer to the King and Monseigneur the Dauphin." Big Thomas, too, one day paid a ceremonial visit to the king at Versailles. The reason for this visit is not known, but history has recorded details of the procession to mark the occasion:

The superb horse which had the honour of carrying the incomparable Thomas was decorated with a prodigious quantity of teeth, strung across, one row after another. A servant carefully led the horse by the reins in case the joy and cries of the people made him too frisky, which would ill become such a solemn ceremony. Big Thomas was wearing new and most extraordinary attire. At the top of his headdress of solid silver was a globe surmounted by a crowing cock . . . while his scarlet costume, in Turkish style, was decorated with teeth, jaws, and precious stones from the Temple.

Large fortunes were made on the Pont-Neuf. A certain man known as the Lyonnaise, who started life as a humble dog-clipper, became official surgeon to the king's pack of hounds. On his retirement, he spent the rest of his days very comfortably on the estate he had bought in Burgundy. Brioché founded a virtual dynasty of puppeteers, whose activities assumed the proportions of a trust company, for they extended into every branch of travelling shows, from the sale of perfumes to the pulling of teeth. The most spectacular success was undoubtedly that of Tabarin. He specialized in the sale of balms and drugs that were very highly thought of, even by the bourgeoisie and the nobility. As was common with all mountebanks, he gave shows with a partner, Mondor. He was not content with small sketches, however, but possessed a real theatre with musicians. He gave daily performances, as well as special shows on Fridays. They became very fashionable and were greatly missed when Tabarin left Paris to tour the provinces. The appearance of this great showman was reason enough for his success: he wore baggy trousers with a wooden sword hanging from his waist. He had a large moustache and the most gigantic hat, which must have contributed a great deal to his popularity, as he used to mould it with his fingers into the most incredible shapes.

One day, having amassed a huge fortune, Tabarin made his final appearance before the Parisian public. Like his partner, Mondor, who became Seigneur of Coteroye and of Frety, he bought a country estate where he planned to spend his final years. His grand and ostentatious style of living, however, antagonized the local gentry, who found it unbearable to see a mere mountebank playing the great lord. They invited him to a hunting party and one of them, having provoked him for the most trifling of reasons, ran his sword through him.

Big Thomas performing his act. (Bibliothèque Nationale, Paris)

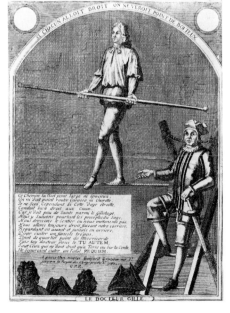

Display of acrobatics. (Bibliothèque Nationale, Paris)

Southwark Fair.
(British Museum,
London)

The Fair of Saint-Germain

The mountebanks owed their success to the quantity rather than the quality of their public, for the well-to-do people driving across the Pont-Neuf in their carriages rarely stopped there. On the other hand, the place was crawling with pages, students, soldiers in search of amusement or fights; idle, curious people; pickpockets. All the servants from the great households of the nobility —footmen, coachmen, servant girls —whenever they were sent out on errands, took advantage of the occasion to scrounge ten minutes or so of their masters' time to loiter for a while on the Pont-Neuf, even if their wages were docked.

In this system of entertainment, at least, payment was optional. The street provided free shows and asked nothing in return. And just because it asked nothing, it was rewarded by the small, sentimental offerings of all those who were grateful to be able to shake off their cares and worries for a few minutes.

At the Fair of Saint-Germain, the public ·was not limited to the common people. It was held in the month of April and, as at the Pont-Neuf, attracted every kind of mountebank. At night, after a ball or an opera, groups of courtiers would congregate there in company with fine ladies wearing masks and exposing their delicate bodies to the pushings and shoving of the crowd. King Henry IV and his queen were regular visitors to the fair. The king even had a box built there where he came every evening to play cards. As the monarchy became more authoritarian, however, the kings gave up this habit. Louis XIV would have considered it beneath his

A nineteenth-century
bear-leader. (Imagerie
Collection)

The Great Charlatan.
(Bibliothèque
Nationale, Paris)

The Charlatan
displays the skin of a
man he has "cured."
(Bibliothèque
Nationale, Paris)

dignity to appear in person among the common people. The royal princes were always there, however, and the Duke of Chartres once arrived at the fair without his shirt because the conjuror Pinette had removed it without the duke being aware of the fact. The aristocracy always had a taste for this kind of entertainment. One might say it was because they enjoyed "slumming," but they were also attracted to the fair because it had a spontaneity and liveliness about it that was totally lacking in the splendid theatrical spectacles given at court. As Oscar Wilde observed, "simple pleasures are the last refuge of complicated natures." Thus, while the common people looked forward impatiently to those rare occasions when they could take part in grandiose festivities, such as the king's entry into a town, the courtiers, in contrast, who saw such events all the time at Versailles, took a far greater delight in watching a conjuror swallowing frogs.

Jodelot   Poisson   Turlupin   LeCapitan» Matamore.   Arlequin.   Guillot Gorju   Gros Guillaume   Le Doctor Grazian Baloard   Polichinelle   Gautier-Garguille   Pantalon.   Philippin.   Briguelle   Trin

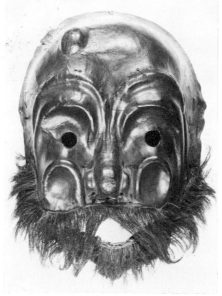

Characters from the commedia dell'arte
—the Captain with his huge plume and
spurs is on the left in the background;
Harlequin is in the middle; Pantaloon
and Punch are at the back on the right
by the wall. They are mingling with
characters from traditional French farce
—Guillot-Gorju is in black behind
Harlequin; Gautier-Garguille is at the
back on the right. On the far left is
Molière, an admirer of the Italian theatre
and one of France's greatest dramatists.
(Comédie Française, Paris)

The mask of one of the zanni, servants
in the commedia dell'arte. *(Opéra
Library, Paris)*

CHAPTER 4

THE COMMEDIA DELL'ARTE

The scene is set around 1560 in a small town in Italy, where the public square fulfils another function besides that of showing off the statues to their best advantage. A company of actors—probably entertainers trained at the stands of the mountebanks—is putting up a stage. The townspeople crowd round in happy anticipation of seeing a comedy. But they are not nearly as overjoyed as the countryfolk who still superstitiously believe that the arrival of actors heralds a long-awaited rainstorm. Apparently they have not yet learned the difference between the words *istrioni* (comedians) and *stregoni* (sorcerers). Instead of rain, of course, they are to see a comedy performed by a troupe specializing in *commedia dell'arte*.

Despite its name, which means "comedy of the professions," *commedia dell'arte* was comedy of such broad appeal that it could be equally enjoyed by rich and poor. A good deal of this appeal rested on the fact that the plays of the *commedia dell'arte* tended towards farce, based on constantly reworked stock situations, portrayed in stock ways, employing stock emotions. In short, the *commedia dell'arte* made no spectacular demands on the intellect of its audiences. It was, on the other hand, enormously demanding for actors for the simple reason that all the plays in the vast repertoire of the *commedia dell'arte* troupes were improvised as they were played. There was no printed dialogue for the actors to memorize. Instead, on the day of the production the producer selected a scenario and posted an outline of it where all the players could read it. A list of necessary props, costumes, and masks was also available. From that point on it was up to the actors to enact convincingly *The Widow's Revenge*, *Harlequin's Hunt for the Missing Donkey*, or whatever the chosen attraction was to be.

In *commedia*, with its absence of script and stage directions, everything depended on the actors, who had to be extraordinarily quick-witted. Their inventiveness provided as much amusement for the audience as the dramas that were enacted. One could easily attend six consecutive performances with the same title and see what amounted to a new play each time. The incredible skill and stage presence of these actors is made only slightly less awe-inspiring when one learns that a certain player often became associated with a particular role and could thus devote a lifetime to its perfection. It is worth investigating some of these stock characters not only because of the part they played in the *commedia* but also because they were the ancestors of characters who

Il Capitan Cocodrillo.　　Harlequin deguisé.　　La Donna Lucia.

Caché de mon manteau, ie sçauray le secret
De ce faux Harlequin q̃ foubs l'habit d'Horace,
Veult ioüir finement & entrer en la grace
De ceste Dame cy, qui l'estime discret.

Ie suis Cheualier & Seigneur estranger,
Arriué d'outre mer pour vo' veoir ma maistresse,
Iamais ne manquerez de biens ny de richesse,
Si voulez comme amy ceste nuict me loger.

Pour vous rendre (monsieur) en ce cas satisfaict
Veu que tãt vous m'aimez, vous aurez ioüissance
De ce que desirez, tout à vostre plaisance,　iij.
Pour l'or & les presens, la femme beaucoup fait.

La Donna Lucia.　　Il Segnor Pantalon　　Zany.

Impudent Pantalon, pense-tu captiuer
Par tes faquins propos, la fleur de ma ieunesse?
Non non, ioindre vn printẽs auec vne vieillesse,
Est faire vn feu flambant à la neige estriuer.

Ma mignône, mon bien, mõ ame, & mon cœur doux,
De vostre pauure Esclaue oyez vne parole,
Ainsi que dict Zany, mon sçauant protecteur,
T'enrageray tout vif, si ne couche auec vous.　ij.

Au diable le poltron, ie n'ay pas dict ainsi,
Voila pour tout gaster, ô la grande pécore,
Pantalon escoutez, recommencez encore,
Et de mieux haranguer prenez tost le saucy.

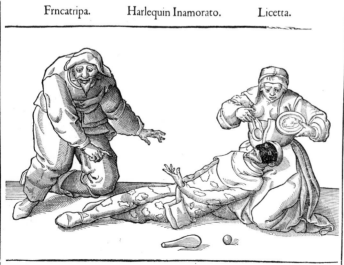

Frncatripa.　　Harlequin Inamorato.　　Licetta.

Messieurs les amoureux, aprochez vous d'icy,
Regardez Harlequin q̃ meurt pour sa maistresse,
Il est plat estendu, pasle, morne, & transi,
Faulte d'auoir donné vn pauure coup de fesse.

Helasic'est faict de moy, ie parle & si suis mort,
Le nautonnier Charon me passe en sa nacelle,
Puis q̃ ma Frãcisquine où gist mon reconfort,
Reiette mes amours, & m'est ainsi cruelle.

Le pauure hôme n'a plus que les os & la peau,
Tant le maudit amour le brusle & le tempeste,
Harlequin mon amy, humez de ce chaudeau,
C'est pour vo' restaurer & refaire la teste.　j.

have become a part of theatrical history. The *commedia* is a deep well of invention from which the contemporary theatre and cinema still draw inspiration.

Pulcinella and Pantaloon

The most important figures in the *commedia* were the *zanni*, or servants, around whom the plot was often woven, and whose actions can be deduced easily as soon as one recognizes the root of the word "zany" in their name. Performing *lazzi* (antics) learned from the mountebanks, which ran the gamut from somersaults to practical jokes, the *zanni* were nearly always lovable, witty and acrobatic. The most famous was Arlecchino, or Harlequin. It indicates at least something about the development of Western culture that in medieval literature a character named Alichino, or Harlequin, often appeared as an impish devil's assistant. From devil's helper to *zanno* to clown—here, perhaps, is a small clue to the evolution of man's diversions! In the *commedia* one of Arlecchino's closest companions was Brighella, a far less lovable type, who was often both cowardly and villainous—ever ready to do anything for a small monetary reward. Nevertheless, in his white costume and black mask, he provided a rich strain for another branch of clowning. His dramatic descendants include, among others, Figaro. Another of the *zanni* was Pedrolino or Pierrot, a lovable daydreamer from whom Pagliaccio and, perhaps, even Charlie Chaplin's bashful heroes were drawn. Still another of these stock figures was Pulcinella, the hunchbacked, skirt-chasing bachelor, better known as the puppet Punch.

Among the leading characters in these plays was Pantalone (Panta-

loon), or *Il Magnifico*, as he was ironically called. A Venetian, his accent alone could be counted on for a few laughs in every town except, of course, the one he was supposed to come from. An elderly man, a tireless talker, busybody, and nuisance to nubile females, Pantalone was a pivot for all kinds of action that revolved around his adventures with young girls, his wife, or even his daughters. Almost always his costume consisted of a red vest, stockings to match, a long black cloak, a woollen cap, and pointed Turkish slippers.

One of his foils was *Il Dottore* (the Doctor), a pedant of unbearable platitudinousness who sprinkled his speeches with garbled Latin phrases. His accent was usually that of Bologna with its famous university—again a cause for laughter elsewhere on the peninsula. His basic stupidity—disguised by his learned accent, Latin, and a majestic doctoral robe with white ruff at the neck—made him the butt of much of the humour.

Still another of the "straight" men in these plays was *Il Capitano* (the Captain), who was usually portrayed as an outsider, one of the hated Spanish or French oppressors. He claimed enormous heroism for himself on fields of battle where he had never been seen. In the course of the play his basic cowardice was nearly always revealed. As an officer and a gentleman, his conviction was that he was the answer to a maiden's prayer, which was about as true as his presumed valour in battle. In time, the captain was replaced in the *commedia* by the far-better-known Scarramuccia, or Scaramouche, and eventually was transformed into a type quite similar to the sympathetic Cyrano de Bergerac. He was a seventeenth-century French author and playwright, who specialized in

satire. He was famed as a swordsman and for his extremely long nose.

Compared to these entertaining characters the lovers, sad to say, were rather dull, although they were presumably the real centre of the action. The lover was usually a matinee-idol type, who spoke in flawless Tuscan, the standard dialect of educated Italians to this day. His beloved was a sweet young thing, but incomparably less entertaining than her servant, and often Arlecchino's darling, Columbine. Bright, clever, and witty, Columbine, of course, eventually became the Pierrette of the French versions of the *commedia dell'arte*. In addition to these basic types, the *commedia*

Opposite top: Harlequin, assisted by the Captain, woos Donna Lucia. Centre: Pantaloon tries to gain entry to Donna Lucia's Castle. Above: Pantaloon in one of his aggressive outbursts is restrained by his valet. Below: Harlequin sets out to conquer the world. Below, left: Harlequin dies of love. All these scenes were favourites in the commedia dell'arte.

also occasionally made use of a ballerina and a *cantarina* to dance and sing—in the unlikely event that the action was not moving along at a sufficiently lively pace.

Harlequin, Emperor of the Moon

Since the *commedia dell'arte* contained all the basic ingredients of universally understandable comedy it did not long remain south of the Alps. It soon became quite natural for travelling companies to ignore national boundaries and to play before foreign audiences.

Their favourite place was Paris, but there they met the hostility of a parliament only too ready to see all theatrical performances as debauchery. To the members of that austere body the theatre contributed to "the ruin of the families of the poor artisans who fill the pit and who, more than two hours before the performance, pass their time with lewd jokes and games of cards and dice that frequently give rise to quarrels and fights." However, thanks to the patronage and protection of some monarchs, who through their marriages to Italian princesses had become familiar with the *commedia dell'arte*, Harlequin and his companions succeeded in establishing themselves in Paris by the end of the sixteenth century.

At first there were communications difficulties, since dialogue did play some part in the Italian theatre. The actors managed to exploit this difficulty to comic effect by using a mixture of French and Italian. But this device was limited. The Italian theatre began to use French more and more. At the same time, influenced by its new environment, it grew much closer to traditional theatre. It abandoned rudimentary scenarios for scripted plays, some of which, like *Harlequin, Emperor of*

the Moon, soon had all Paris rushing to the theatre. In this play Harlequin described all the wickedness, baseness, and absurdity of an imaginary empire on the moon while the other actors, circling round, cried, lifting their arms to heaven, "Just like here! Just like here!" Soon the Italian theatre had a real repertoire. The stage sets, the acting, even the costumes, became more refined. Harlequin's costume, for example, originally composed of bits and pieces sewn together with no regard for colour, a real poor devil's old rags, soon became a harmonious ensemble of triangles or diamonds outlined with yellow braid—a real pleasure to behold.

Social satire

But although it developed, the *commedia dell'arte* did not deny its origins. It kept its traditional characters, its skilful use of gestures and improvisation, and above all the verve and the feeling for dialogue that struck straight at the root of things, which it inherited from its popular origins. Spontaneity and conciseness were the fundamental qualities of this kind of theatre. "Let us condense a whole satire into one bold and lively epigram," wrote the French author Alain René Lesage later, explaining that Italian theatre must not on any account attempt to imitate literary theatre.

The spirit remained the same, but its scope was now wider and more subtle. Daily life was no longer the only target for their satire. The barbs now were hurled at a society where authority was becoming increasingly burdensome, and more particularly at financiers and the forces of justice. In seventeenth-century France the two were sometimes confused, since the judges, who had to purchase their offices, gained back the price later

ARLEQUIN EMPEREUR DANS LA LUNE

Gillot inv.

Huquier Sculp. ex.

A commedia dell'arte troupe, probably Gelosi's. (Carnavalet Museum, Paris)

with the bribes they demanded from the litigants. This is the Italian theatre's version of the advice given by a veteran to a new judge: "The secret of the profession, its great achievement and the reason for its success, lies in the writing: don't be so naïve as to attend hearings; send notes and counter-notes, multiply the legal difficulties, and above all never, on any pretext, consent to a final sentence. For the rest, if you like money, you're already halfway to being a judge." "You see, my dear boy," says Pettifog to his pupil, "I speak as a father in showing you the inner workings of our profession."

As for Mr Resourceful, notary, he puts before his clients several proved models of how to go bankrupt, "For a good father has a moral duty to go bankrupt at least once in his life for the sake of his children."

The financier Mouldy explains this lengthily to his wife when, faced with ruin, he has had the good fortune to meet Mr Resourceful:

"How lucky we are, my dear, to have fallen into the hands of such an honest man! Come now, my love! I am sure heaven will back us up, since we only want to give our children a good start and to live quietly for the rest of our lives in a manner befitting our station."

The procedure devised by Mr Resourceful is simple: it is enough to live in a grand style, borrowing enormous sums of money, and then to disappear quietly and wait until the creditors enter into a contract agreeing to renounce two-thirds of the sum lent in order to get back the remainder. "A man who has taken this prudent step once in his life will always be beforehand with the world."

The disastrous publicity stunt

The Italian theatre's attacks on justice and the police seemed violent because there was no precautionary speech to tone down their effect, as there was in more literary works

where satires on justice had become commonplace. Harlequin declared: "Attorney, thief, is like saying barber, wigmaker: the one presupposes the other"—which does not evidence any great mastery of insinuation. Elsewhere police commissioners were treated as rogues and gaolbirds, and it was baldly stated that they would arrest anyone if bribed to do so.

It should be noted, however, that the actors were attacking the subordinate representatives of authority. In their plays it was the middle classes who were satirized, not the court and still less the king's immediate circle, so that the annoyances and harassment the actors met never went very far. But it was otherwise when they blundered into a satirical attack aimed directly at the royal household. Then the axe fell.

Before recounting this episode, a few explanations are in order. King Louis XIV, who was always very well disposed towards the Italian

theatre, secretly took Madame de Maintenon as his second wife. Everyone disliked this austere woman who imposed an atmosphere of puritanism and piety on the court. A novel entitled *The Perfidious Prude*, which had appeared in Holland, was banned in France because of its allusions to Madame de Maintenon. Of course, all Paris was soon secretly talking about it.

Bravely, perhaps to settle with an officious queen who had often picked quarrels with them, but also no doubt to get easy publicity, the Italian actors gave to the play originally advertised as *The Perfidious Mother-in-Law* a new title, *The Perfidious Prude*. The theatre was packed. But the actors were awakened early the next morning: an army of commissioners headed by a police lieutenant had come to announce the closing of their theatre. They were forbidden henceforth to perform within a thirty-league radius of Paris. Once more society had made certain that its artists did not

Descendants of Harlequin were widespread in nineteenth-century circuses and stage shows. (Opéra Library, Paris)

become middle class; they became vagabonds again.

The Italian actors were not the only ones to regret their daring. Many writers and men of letters had haunted the Italian theatre. Montaigne and Molière apart, a classicist like Boileau, who was considered gravity incarnate, was a great admirer of the *commedia dell'arte*. This is understandable, for these popular shows had in abundance something one does not always find elsewhere: truth, action, life. As President de Brosses later remarked, "The acting at the Italian theatre has a quite different realism, a quite different air of truth, than the spectacle at the Théâtre Français of four or five actors standing in a row, like a bas-relief, speaking their lines each in turn."

There was also a bracing farcical lyricism, which was excellent in its own way. For example, here is the Captain recounting a vulgar beating:

"Today some flunkeys finding me
    alone,
Beat me lengthily and hard
But this insult incensed me so
I devoured the walls of a boule-
    vard
Swollen with vexation and ran-
    cour soon
I battered furtune
Scorched chance and set light to
    ill luck.
Raging amuck"

A monopoly

While the actors who had been chased out of Paris were touring the provinces looking for an audience, itinerant companies whose sense of literary and artistic copyright was not too acute were quietly taking over their repertoire in Paris. This happened in the fairground at Saint-Germain where, as we saw earlier, the world of actors met that of the mountebanks.

But in France at that time the financial regulations introduced by Jean-Baptiste Colbert did not end at the ill-defined frontiers of art. A royal edict gave the Comédie Française the sole right to stage theatrical performances in Paris. This monopoly would not, perhaps, have led to any great consequences if the Comédie's coffers had been full. But they were empty. And the growing success of the Fairground Theatre (as the reincarnated Italian theatre was called at the beginning of the seventeenth century) clashed at once with an irreducible opposition on the part of the official theatre, which possessed some formidable weapons.

It is strange to see artists protecting their production by forbidding anyone to produce. The Comédie Française did this. It did not consider the merits of the respective performances, but asked the forces of justice to protect its privilege, sent commissioners, had the wooden theatres where the actors staged their shows torn down, or even burned. But the actors thought up all sorts of ruses to get round the law, which in essence prohibited the performance of plays with dialogue. For example, they had each character leave the stage at top speed as soon as he had spoken his lines; the dialogue thus became a *monologue*. The public howled with delight every time an actor rushed for the wings, his words hardly out of his mouth. So the monologue had to be banned. Then the actors tried singing. They had managed to buy from a director of the opera, which was crippled with debts, permission to sing their lines instead of speaking them (the opera had the sole right to sing on the banks of the Seine). But this authorization, which the actors had purchased on a yearly basis, was illegal. It, too, was taken away from them. There remained only mime and jargon, that is, inarticulate sounds, which they exploited to the full by parodying the declamatory style of the great tragedies. It was funny, but rather limited. They had to invent another way of speaking without using their voices. They fell back on scrolls on which the lines were written in large letters and which the actors, at the right moment, produced from their pockets to show the audience. But the real stroke of genius was in a refinement of this trick: they thought of getting the audience, not the actors, to sing the lines that they were not allowed to say on stage. Two violinists would strike up a well-known tune, and the whole house, spurred on by a few collaborators planted in the audience, would take up the song:

> "How fortunate are the burghers
>   of Paris
> When their Plume wings to Glory!
> Of the Fair Sex they are all be-
>   loved,
> How fortunate are the burghers
>   of Paris!"

In this way the spectators became actors, and the Italian theatre rediscovered the popular vein from which it arose. There was a real complicity between audience and actors without which they could not have resisted the harassment they encountered. But this complicity did not end with the show. In France, where a revolutionary tide was rising at the time, the masses felt a solidarity with these actors, who, lacking everything, managed through their ingenuity to vanquish an authority whose iniquities became daily more flagrant. At the Fairground Theatre they had the feeling of laughing with justice on

their side. In contrast, at the carnivals to which we now turn our attention, everyone simply enjoyed life and laughter for a brief moment, without a single thought for any great moral precepts.

The affair of La Fausse Prude (The Perfidious Prude). *The Italian actors are driven off the day after their performance. (Le Havre Museum)*

CHAPTER 5

CARNIVALS

The Feast of Fools, with all its excesses, was in essence a parody of much more ancient festivals that are known as carnivals. The Feast of Fools was acted out according to a well-defined framework and followed an etiquette that was decided upon in advance. A carnival, on the other hand, suggests boundless delirium, revelry, parody, games, disguises, frenzy, and pageantry. It is the most characteristic of popular festivals.

Throughout history carnivals have been closely associated with the cycle of the seasons. The Egyptians celebrated a spring festival with carnival spirit in honour of their god of fertility, Osiris, who was associated with the annual flooding of the Nile and the renewed richness of the land. The Greeks began to celebrate a similar event in honour of the god Dionysus in about the sixth century BC. A modern visitor would have felt perfectly at home at a Greek carnival with its floats winding through the narrow streets and the unbounded merrymaking that marked the holiday. The Romans with their love of celebration carried on these ancient carnivals—and multiplied them. Lupercalia, their fertility carnival, was held in February. Although it originated as a rustic festival aimed at ensuring good crops, Lupercalia came to be a time when humans sought fertility as well. Two boys dressed as he-goats ran a fixed course through Rome, lightly lashing whoever passed with goatskins. Women eagerly took their places along the course to receive the lash of fertility. Saturnalia, which was held in December, began as a country custom, too, and honoured the autumn planting. As we have noted earlier, it became a period when slaves briefly enjoyed both freedom and being served by their masters. Since it was also a time for gift-giving and celebrating, Saturnalia may be one of the roots of our own Christmas traditions. The lustiest and most ribald of all Roman carnivals was Bacchanalia, in honour of the wine god, Bacchus. But things apparently grew too rowdy at these carnivals and they were outlawed in the second century BC.

The spirit of these ancient carnivals honouring dimly remembered gods persisted well into the Christian era, as the Feast of Fools testifies. Gradually, however, the Church managed to contain all the wild spirit of these old festivals in the period before the beginning of Lent. The word "carnival" itself derives from the old Italian *carnelevare*— lifting of the meat—and is most closely associated with the fasting of the Lenten season. Today, however, any local festival, small circus,

Opposite: Carnival on the Place de la Concorde, Paris, by Seigneurgens.

or joyous celebration may be called a carnival.

The cats go to the Sabbath

As we have seen, country carnivals originally marked the end of an unproductive period and a return to fertility. The people banished winter, they chased it away. In order to emphasize the solemn character of this rupture, they represented winter symbolically as fantastic or hideous creatures through the puppets that accompanied the dancing and that were destroyed at the end of the festival. In some areas the symbolic nature of this show was particularly clear. In Alsace, for example, winter appeared as a puppet dressed in straw; it was dragged through the streets at the end of a rope, abused, beaten, and finally drowned in a pond. Elsewhere, winter was represented by masks similar to those worn in primitive civilizations or, as in Württemberg and many other parts of Germany, appeared as a witch: its decrepitude, its ugliness, symbolized the accursed season. Today at Imst, in a valley in the Tyrol, one can still see the witches' dance at a carnival that has remained scrupulously faithful to a timeless tradition.

Local superstitions became attached to the universal theme. The people of Touraine believed that on the night of Shrove Tuesday the Cats' Sabbath was held, presided over by a big tomcat playing a violin. But as they drink hard in Touraine during this festive time, the popular proverb adds, "The cats go to the Sabbath, but no one's able to see them."

The custom, characteristic of carnivals, of sprinkling water and throwing all sorts of things, soot and flour, for example, in each other's face, may be attributed to old fertility rites. But the history of confetti is still to be traced: it is doubtless full of surprises. For example, in sixteenth-century Rome the people bombarded each other with eggs. The eggs were emptied, without breaking the shell, by boring two holes in one end and then were filled with sand. But as the eggs were expensive, turnips were also used. The custom of throwing sugared almonds developed later. As the frenzy of the Rome Carnival necessitated enormous quantities of small projectiles, they were devised *ad hoc*. Small balls of plaster may be the ancestors of our confetti.

The scapegoat

But, despite the bucolic and pagan overtones, Western carnivals were inseparable from the Christian custom of fasting and self-deprivation that accompanied Lent. Today these practices are fully observed only rarely, but in Charlemagne's time violation of the fast was punishable by death. This severity was mitigated in time. Later, the offenders were simply exhibited or walked through the streets with a joint of meat hung round their necks. Eventually dispensations were given, but these gave rise to barter and fraud so the civil authorities began to check their validity and to exercise closer surveillance.

The carnival that preceded the dark days of Lenten deprivation took on the aspect of a revenge in anticipation. Food, abundance, and mess played a fundamental role in these festivities. In many parts of France the carnival character who dominated the procession was a pot-bellied fellow, absurdly sensual, a sort of joyful and vaguely ridiculous giant. But not a repellent one, as the people of Ariège used to sing.

"Carnival's an honest fellow
But a wee bit greedy
Stuffing too much in his belly
He bursts while still feeding."

This character was destroyed on the morning of Ash Wednesday, but not before a solemn burlesque trial had been held at which he was accused of being a drunkard and a lecher who had brought his family to ruin. The way he was put to death varied from one district to another: he was burned, drowned and even in some places impaled and riddled with bullets. Why this cruelty? Obviously because this symbolic character was a scapegoat on whom were piled all the sins of the community, all the excesses committed during the festival, and

perhaps during the rest of the year.

The obsession with food, which was fostered by Lent, was characteristic of a civilization where hunger ruled. In Naples during the eighteenth century it appeared in a particularly spectacular form. A "Feast Theatre" was built out of all kinds of food, and on top our old friend the god Saturn was enthroned. At the appointed time a cannon roared, and a huge crowd attacked the edifice. Certain cultural preoccupations inherited from ancient times were curiously mixed with the orgy of eating. The "theatre" with bread walls represented the temple of Aphrodite, or the city of Troy besieged by the Greeks. As a result one observer remarked very seriously, "I find it admirable that in a

IL TRIOMFO DEL CARNEVAL

DI VENECIA APPRESSO
LVDOVICO NILETTI

public entertainment, the lowest class of society, I mean that which generally learns nothing, should know that there has been a city of Troy, and that this city was besieged." But it is open to doubt whether the participants took a historic view of the subtleties of their architecture.

A drunken populace

As a distinguished nineteenth-century scholar wrote in a treatise on carnivals:

Apparently at this time of general delirium, all feelings were suspended, all memories were held in abeyance; no one remembered the domestic troubles, the family problems, the inevitable sufferings of life. The poor forgot their poverty, and even the sick forgot their pain. Carnivals, like any other festival in the fullest sense of the word, were in effect a negation of daily life. Each individual became omnipotent in relation to himself and to others. His rule of conduct was excess: of this eating and dancing were the most obvious indications. The reserve that usually controlled his relations with his fellows no longer existed: he covered them with soot, sprayed them with revolting and variably picturesque substances. The hypocrisy, which in general governed social relations, gave way to satire and mockery. As the proverb says, "At the beginning of Lent and grape-harvest time, you're allowed to say anything."

In small communities the people attacked their neighbours, jeered at their private lives, exposed their conjugal grievances in the public

An obsession with food is an integral part of carnivals. This procession illustrates the point well. (Opéra Library, Paris)

square. This occurred almost everywhere. At Bâie it took the form of organized duels, battles of wit in which home truths were delivered.

Carnivals were thus a negation of the principles on which daily intercourse, the whole social order, in the wide sense of the term, was based. Like the Feast of Fools, they presented a topsy-turvy world, a reality typified by the Lunatics' Chariot, which seems to have been customary at the Rome Carnival, as it is found in descriptions and illustrated documents. On this chariot, it was the lunatics who kept the keys to the asylum. And the topsy-turvy world naturally entailed the abolition of prohibitions, starting with those protecting hearth and home. In many places it was customary for the people in the carnival procession, or even anyone at all, to go into houses and take variably pleasing liberties and, if masked, they were not always obliged to reveal their identity to the master of the house. Even the taboos against gratuitous and spectacular destruction came under attack, and goodness knows these were strong! At Binche, in Belgium, it was customary to throw oranges at houses. Too bad for the windows and the things inside! For a long time the inhabitants of Binche took the precaution of putting railings in front of their windows at the start of the carnival.

The dummy patriarch

Besides these customs, which have a universal meaning, carnivals were associated with a host of surprising ceremonies deriving from particular events in local history. For example, on Maundy Thursday St Mark's Square was the scene of a strange ritual attended by everyone in Venice. Platforms were erected on which the doge and the aristocracy

took their places. Then, to the sound of fanfares, a bull was led forward and its head cut off with a sword. This exploit was carried out by the guild of butchers. Afterwards, surrounded by exploding fireworks, mountebanks climbed up to the bell-tower of St Mark's.

The interest of this custom of beheading a bull lies less in its strangeness than in the historical event that gave rise to it. In 1611 the patriarch Aquileia pillaged the town of Gradus. Venice, which was in alliance with this town, organized a punitive expedition against the patriarch. He was defeated, captured, and imprisoned in Venice. Later he was released—but under one strange condition. Every year on Maundy Thursday, the anniversary of his defeat, he had to send to Venice one bull and twelve pigs, on which the magistrates solemnly renewed the sentence of death that should have fallen on the patriarch. The substitution of animals of doubtful nobility for the patriarch revealed a deliberate intention of humiliating him. After this ceremony the doge with his staff destroyed some miniature fortresses erected in the palace courtyard, as a sign of the fate that awaited the enemies of the republic. This latter

custom disappeared fairly quickly, but that of beheading the bull lasted into the eighteenth century.

The masqueraders' kingdom

But the interest of the Venice Carnival lies above all in the fact that it was not, like those previously mentioned, a brief, frantic period of merrymaking lasting only a few days. It became a real "season," almost a way of life. It lasted from the beginning of January until Lent, and started up again now and then in spring and autumn. When a doge died during this period, the news was kept secret so as not to interrupt the festivities.

The carnival owed its success in part to the wealth and luxury of seventeenth-century Venice, where the women were said to spend hours grooming their hair so as to make it shine like gold, and where, periodically, sumptuary laws were passed and, of course, not observed. This is not surprising since Venice, like ancient Rome, could not have staged its grandiose shows if it had not drained all the riches of the Mediterranean. But there was one particular reason for the success of the Venice Carnival: the absence of traffic created favourable conditions for the festival by giving the crowd invading the town complete freedom of movement.

The crowd, of course, was formed of masqueraders entering and coming out of the houses, meeting in groups and chasing each other.

Although domino shapes were generally worn, the masks were of all patterns and colours. Animals' heads, realistic masks, and stylized ones, evoking a burlesque version of the monsters painted by Hieronymus Bosch, mixed naturally with the innumerable characters of the *commedia dell'arte*. Pulcinella walked beside exaggeratedly dignified doctors; Columbine, besieged by a group of coachmen, escaped on the arm of a Shakespearean ghost. Some disguised themselves "back to front," so that they seemed to be walking backwards, probably inspired by Dante's "punishment" of fortune tellers in Hell, but it was an unnerving spectacle to behold by the side of a canal. Others, like the ass and the turkey walking hand in hand, formed carefully composed groups that looked like the characters of a picture that had stepped out of their frame. This carnival was a feast for the eyes, an ever-changing spectacle as much as a festival. It was an urbanized, civilized, refined carnival, far removed from the rustic rituals. In Venice there was a mask industry comparable in its organization and number of workers to the other artisans' guilds.

The masqueraders were not only in disguise, but also incognito. This gave rise to a game; you never knew

who had come to sit next to you and was engaging you in conversation. The chance to live incognito was the soul of the Venice Carnival, and even its legal definition, since the carnival was held on the days when disguises were permitted. In this respect, there was a revealing custom called the *segno di maschera*, a distinctive sign, usually a miniature domino pinned to the hat, which gave the wearer the right to anonymity. Anyone wearing it was regarded as being masked. He was not to be greeted and if, as was often the case, the person wearing the sign was someone of importance, no special respect was shown when addressing him. He could be tapped familiarly on the shoulder. This convention enabled people to lay down the burden of their official personality: masks, even symbolic ones, wiped away social hierarchies.

It was in St Mark's Square that the masqueraders came to show

Masks were to be found all over Venice, even in gaming-rooms. (Carrara Academy, Bergamo)

themselves off in a promenade called the *listone*. The aristocracy came to admire the original inventions. On these evenings some forty thousand people were to be found in and around the square. Afterwards the crowd went off to dances and plays, for the carnival opened a season of uninterrupted shows.

The refinements of the Venice Carnival reached other Italian cities, particularly Rome, where for a long time the occasion had been celebrated only by rather rough amusements. One of these was a race between old men who ran naked down the Via del Corso: the winner was awarded a much-needed piece of material, the *palio*.

Pope Paul II, who came to Rome from Venice in the fifteenth century, was the first to introduce the splendours of his native town into these ceremonies.

The infamous masquerade of Nantes

The Venice Carnival was a model for all Europe. From the eighteenth century on, balls became very fashionable in every city, and especially in Paris. There the Opéra Ball attracted a rather motley crowd, among whom, however, a clear distinction was drawn by the fact that the boxes were reserved for the aristocracy. Only the passages and foyer were open to the public.

With these balls spread the custom of masking oneself as in Venice, that is as a social art practised aesthetically and satirically, not, as in rustic ceremonies, to symbolize malevolent forces. But in Venice the satirical use of masks was subject to quite strict laws: it was forbidden to take advantage of the occasion to ridicule the authorities.

Right: a staircase in the Opéra during the Carnival Ball, by Gustave Doré. (Opéra Library, Paris)

Below: The Carnival *by Debucourt.* (Bibliothèque Nationale, Paris)

These laws, written or otherwise, were not always understood in provincial towns where, as no tradition yet controlled these recently introduced customs, there was a naive belief that everything was allowed. Such was the case in Nantes on 7 February 1745. At one of the balls in the town on that evening there was an apothecary who pursued those present with a syringe. Not everybody found this parody of a venerable body in good taste, but things got much worse when someone else appeared in a disguise which, without being precisely that of a monk, still evoked unambiguously the Brotherhood of Igorantine Friars. And as everyone in Nantes had ideas that day, two "turks" soon arrived, a man and a woman, who at once caused a considerable stir. Their abnormally chubby masks looked more like behinds than faces. These people who, without knowing it, were resurrecting the Feast of Fools, invited ladies to dance, and walked round asking those present if their joke was in good taste. Most replies were negative. There were mutterings of condemnation, then hostility. The police were called. The jokers vanished.

There was a scandal in the town. Everywhere it was rumoured that the masks had been made by a man called Lesueur, a sculptor by trade. The police opened an inquiry. It dragged on. It was also whispered that the authors of the "infamous masquerade" were not without influence in the town. Names circulated, but no one took the responsibility of quoting them in public. Faced with the negligence of the police, the Church stepped in. A fortnight later a priest, from his pulpit, threatened excommunication to any person who had some knowledge of the scandal and did not disclose it immediately. This ancient threat did what the police had been unable to do: tongues were loosened. Perhaps people had been longing to speak out. Lesueur was arrested and made a dramatic confession. The guilty parties were brought to justice. The trial however did not turn out badly: the sentences were light.

Committee carnivals

We will see later what remains today of traditional carnivals. Let us say at once, however, that by the nineteenth century they had greatly dwindled in number and in spirit. True, at almost all periods there were laments that festivals had declined. In the middle of the eighteenth century a beautiful Englishwoman wrote: "During these amusements [at carnivals] no one is amused. In Amsterdam they write, in Venice they play, in Paris they yawn, and in London they sleep. It is only in Rome that they run mad, but the Pope does not permit this to last more than a week."

However, it is quite possible that this lady was yielding to the temptation to be witty. The universal lamentation of nineteenth-century festival-lovers is more serious. They complained that the masks were degenerating, were becoming ugly and standardized, and they decried what they called "committee carnivals," organized by the municipal authorities whose aesthetic sense was no more beyond reproach than their sense of tradition. The heavy, solemn processions that emerged from their deliberations were contrary to the spirit of the ancient carnival, in which the procession had no intrinsic value, but was only a rallying point for the collective "madness." The towns neglected their festivals. But they had compensations.

A masquerade in Basle. (Opéra Library, Paris)

CHAPTER 6

THE CIRCUS

The circus marked the triumph of the show over the festival. It was not a matter of chance that it became popular in the nineteenth century at the time of the Industrial Revolution. Towns gathered together their troubadours, counted up their mountebanks, and installed them in palaces flooded with light, where the sounding brass, the horsemen's uniforms, the immaculate, solemn costumes of the women riders, and the motley habit of the clowns made up a world of movement and colour that was to be an inexhaustible source of pleasure.

For the circus, according to the nineteenth-century French poet Théophile Gautier, is an "ocular" show—today we would call it a visual feast. This new show followed its own rules, unfolding with the rapidity of a dream, magic following magic in a brilliant display. There were no slack moments to break the enchantment that left the spectator stunned and delighted, at the mercy of the marvellous surprises passing before his eyes.

Astley's Amphitheatre

The first modern circuses were travelling tent shows that were set up at fairs or in country towns. The real pioneer of the circus as we know it was an English ex-soldier, Philip Astley, who set up his circus in London in the late eighteenth century, after having twice tried in vain to establish it in Paris. Seeing the success of his shows, entrepreneurs on the Continent had regrets, and decided to follow suit. Franconi established the Cirque Olympique in Paris and Victor de Bach set up the Circus Gymnasticus in the Prater in Vienna.

The programme of these early circuses consisted mostly of equestrian exercises, dancing on the slack wire, acrobatics, dressage, and acrobatic riding. The events were presented like a military parade with uniforms and fanfare: circuses at that time were closely connected with the army, whose fascination they vulgarized.

In provincial towns the travelling circuses even often used the army training grounds in the neighbourhood to present their shows.

But this succession of equestrian exercises and a few numbers by tightrope-walkers and dancers soon became monotonous. Astley had the idea of introducing burlesque scenes into the show to remedy this deficiency. It was then that clowns appeared. They originally portrayed peasants—blockheads incapable of getting on to a horse or of staying on it properly. Pantomimes were also introduced, and eventually relegated the equestrian exercises to second place. Twentieth-century cir-

Opposite: The Circus by Seurat. *(Jeu de Paume Museum, Paris)*

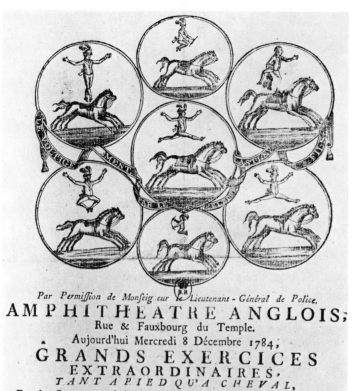

AMPHITHEATRE ANGLOIS;
Rue & Fauxbourg du Temple.
Aujourd'hui Mercredi 8 Décembre 1784,
GRANDS EXERCICES
EXTRAORDINAIRES,
TANT A PIED QU'A CHEVAL,
Par les SIEURS ASTLEY, & la TROUPE ANGLOISE;
Demain Jeudi 9, & après demain Vendredi 10,
PLUSIEURS EXERCICES
Qui feront annoncés dans les Affiches & Billets à la main.
On ouvrira à cinq heures, & on commencera à six précifes.
Premieres Loges 3 livres, Secondes 36 fols, Troijiemes, 24 fols, & Quatriemes 12 fols.
On prie très-humblement de ne point amener des chiens au Manège cela empêcheroit le Spectacle.

At the end of the eighteenth century, Philip Astley, who invented the circus, tried unsuccessfully to introduce his entertainment in Paris. (Bibliothèque Nationale, Paris)

cular comic qualities of clowns could not be conveyed by a collection of the gags and farcical situations that they invented; it would scarcely rise above the level of an anthology of jokes. It is impossible to re-create the atmosphere, especially of the entrance whose effect is achieved by surprise, often that of a simple gesture. The American clown Dan Rice is said to have made the audience laugh as soon as he appeared (wearing a scarecrow's costume and a superb white hat) simply by the way in which he hummed a catch phrase.

On the other hand, there are many types of clowns whose styles can be classified in a rough way. There are acrobatic clowns whose classic number consists of jumping from a springboard over a line of horses, a trick known as the *batoude*. The most famous of these acrobatic clowns was Boswell, who climbed a ladder, removing the rungs one by one, and when he reached the top, turned upside down on one of the uprights, an exercise during which he collapsed one night. Others, like Rice, never open their mouths, and use only gestures. Then there are talking clowns. These are, like most of the others, English—it has been calculated that out of every twenty clowns, fifteen are English. They were called talking clowns or jesters because their act, which resembled that of the court jester, had certain literary overtones.

cuses do not use this type of entertainment because it has been killed by television. It consisted not just of mimed shows but of scenes telling a story or historical reconstructions for which they used the circus's characteristic resources—horses, and later wild animals.

Clowns

In one of the clown Foottit's most famous entrances he entered the arena sitting the wrong way round in the saddle, saying in a tone of dreamy inquiry, "This horse hasn't got a head."

"It's on the other side," remarked the ringmaster.

"Then put it back in the right place," replied Foottit. The parti-

Clowns and Augustes

The most popular form of clowning has been that of the red-nosed *auguste* whose appearance in the ring has given rise to a host of stories. They say that one day Tom Belling, nicknamed Auguste, tripped while leaving the ring because he had drunk too much gin. The ringmaster cursed him, but he replied only with the drunkard's blissful and stupid mimicry. He was kicked on the behind, and the audience howled with laughter. A few days later, with a clear head, Auguste repeated this routine, which had met with such success. This story may not be gospel truth, but it throws into relief the profundities of the *auguste's* character: the incompetent fellow who busies himself around the ring at random, getting in the way of others at work, the idiot who goes beyond the permitted limits of idiocy, but also the poor devil who gets kicked and sworn at.

Buffoonery is not the clown's only sphere. There is real emotion when, abandoning farce, he hands us over to the power of the violin. There is also fear, which the clown Foottit was able to exploit in a remarkable fashion. He exercised over Chocolate, his partner, who had all the characteristics of the *auguste*, a subtle and implacable tyranny. "You've no money, so you're not thirsty," he would say to him, thrusting a gimlet into his ear to overcome his deafness. This provoked laughter that was not as ingenuous as that caused by buffoonery. We laugh at these terrible vexations, although we are sometimes plagued by them in real life. That is why this typical clown exercises a fascination over us.

Of course, it is a much more difficult field than farce. Foottit realized this to his cost. He was very successful at the Nouveau Cirque in the sketches in which he tyrannized Chocolate. But when he left this circus for the suburbs, his shows were a fiasco. Was this because the comic subtlety was lost on a less refined audience? Or is it, as Mr Tristan Rémy believes, because for a working-class public with an extreme sensitivity to certain aspects of

The circus in Paris during the Second Empire. (After Provost, Bibliothèque Nationale, Paris)

The Champs Elysées circus by Valentin. (Bibliothèque Nationale, Paris)

TONY GRICE ORIGINAL ENGLISH CLOWN

L'ORIGINAL WALTER BELLONINI

JONGLEUR EQUILIBRIST AND Exentrique Clown

This page: the marvel of English clowns. (Opéra Library, Paris)

Right: presenting a group of original numbers. (Opéra Library, Paris)

existence, "the relations between master and servant could not be a subject for merriment?"

The psychology of lion-taming

There are two ways of getting wild animals to act in the ring: gently and ferociously. The first consists of making the animal perform "turns" quite contrary to its natural instincts, fawning on the tamer, or allowing him to put his head in its mouth, a feat perfected by animal-trainers in ancient Rome. The second is the more subtle, and perhaps the more spectacular: the tamer provokes and irritates the animal, forcing it by threats to go through an act whose interest consists of tension and suspense. The classic form of this technique consists of a simulated attack. The tamer calls the animal with a snap of his whip, retreats before its attack, then, when the animal is rushing on him with all the signs of anger, he in turn attacks and, whip in hand, leads the animal to the bars where he forces it to stand on its hind legs, roaring and furious. In this kind of show the tamer pretends to threaten, and the lion pretends to attack: it must never pounce in earnest. This is a game.

But the game obeys certain laws, which Henri Thétard, an ex-tamer turned journalist, has explained. If

ORPHEUM

PLACE DE LA RÉPUBLIQUE
10

the EQUILIBRIST

FRUTON JOHNSONLEE
the Original black FRUTON

Lith. CH. LEVY, 4, R. Bouchardon, PARIS (10)

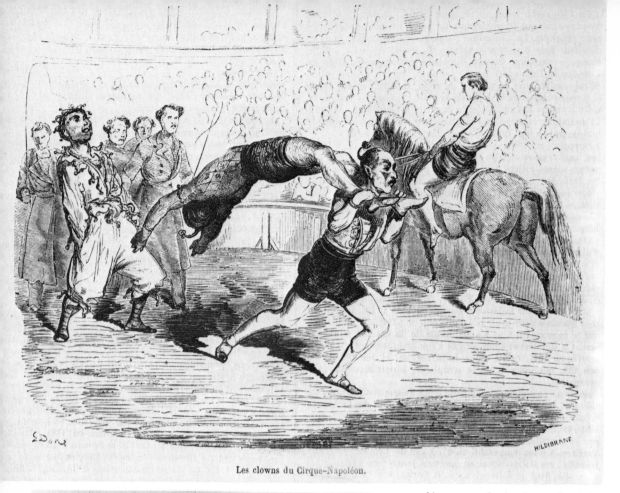

Les clowns du Cirque-Napoléon.

Above: acrobatic clowns from the Napoleon Circus. (Opéra Library, Paris)

Left: in a classical turn, the trainer opens the lion's jaws. (Bibliothèque Nationale, Paris)

Opposite above and below: the tame . . . and the terrible.

the animal retreats it is because fear of the tamer is a conditioned reflex that it has acquired during the decisive confrontation of their first encounters. When the tamer enters the cage for the first time, after having familiarized himself with the animal through the bars, he has attached to one arm a large latticed shield and in the other hand he carries a fork. If the animal attacks, he hits it on the nose—a sensitive point—with the fork, taking care to keep his back to the bars so as not to be taken by surprise from behind. Leopards, for example, do not attack their enemy from the front, instead they jump on to the bars, and from there on to the tamer's shoulders. When the animal has been hit on the nose with the fork, it retreats and, usually, retires growl-

The ferocious . . .

. . . and the docile.

ing to the back of the cage. But if the animal tries to attack again, it meets the same reception. In this way it is conditioned to fear the man who, in the ring, has only to sketch a threatening gesture to make it retreat.

As a matter of principle, hitting is used only in the event of an attack: it is avoided during the real training that starts after the animal submits. And the punishment must be brief, otherwise the tamer "blocks" the animal and establishes with it a relationship of mistrust and hatred that threatens to break out one day into a trial of strength, which is precisely what must be avoided. The tamer must make himself feared and, by giving rewards, accepted; he must not make himself hated.

How to get on with each other

These first contacts are, therefore, decisive. Each species, of course, has its own character. Bears, despite their propensity to adopting comic attitudes, are sly, spiteful, and fight to the end when they attack. They cannot be turned away from their victims by being confronted with some sort of obstacle, a ploy that sometimes works with big cats. The big cats are more prone to bluster than to harbour resentment. Lions give a warning when they are about to attack—by flattening their ears and straightening their tails. Tigers, on the other hand, gather themselves together and leap straight on the man.

Every novice animal-tamer knows

these facts. The great thing, when the trainer enters the cage, is to understand the "subject," the individual confronting him, to recognize incorrigibly stubborn animals, or ones whose past has rendered them untrainable; and, in the case of a healthy animal, to recognize its fears, its dislikes, its phobias, and its lusts. A gesture that would scarcely rouse a growl from one lion may cause another to launch a ferocious attack. One must be aware of these details of personality because an unexpected reaction is the worst danger. This knowledge of the animal allows the tamer to play on its psychological peculiarities. A famous lion-tamer named Martin replied to the novelist Honoré de Balzac's questions about his skill at animal-training by saying, "It is wrong to believe I have secrets. I strive to understand the character of each subject, to pander to its passions. I give rest to the lazy, I play with the playful. I become their friend because they are afraid of having me as an enemy. . . ."

Teaching a lion to sit on a stool is a matter of technique and patience, just as it is to teach the same trick to fifteen lions. The ability to work in the ring with groups of animals, as developed by the renowned German trainer Hagenbeck, demands above all, on the part of the tamer, skilled tactics beyond those we have already mentioned.

Danger!

The tamer's ascendancy is based on very reasonable techniques that few animals resist. One is tempted to believe that if he is not needlessly clumsy or cruel, the tamer runs scarcely any risk.

This is not so. However able the trainer is, however docile the animal appears to be, there is always danger. For example, when the animals are sexually excited they tend to return to a state of instinctive, unsubdued aggression. And, because there are accidents, the animal overwhelmed by sudden fear or pain may no longer recognize its trainer. From this moment on the whole psychological system on which their relationship is based collapses, and the animal attacks. There is always the danger, too, that the animal may attack when it feels that it has the tamer at its mercy—as when his back is turned, or his attention has lapsed. And how can one avoid turning one's back when working with fifteen lions?

The annals of circus history are filled with terrible tales to prove that even the most seemingly docile animals may forget what they have learned—with disastrous consequences. In 1846, van Amburg, one of the most famous lion-tamers in the history of the circus, was appearing in Boston after a triumphant tour of Europe. That evening, the whole menagerie was filled with a sense of excitement. When he entered the ring to get his tigress Edith to perform, she refused to obey. Edith was considered a very docile animal that he had trained without difficulty, without even needing to hit her. Faced with this sudden revolt, van Amburg decided to confront the animal, to cut short any future impulse of resistance. He walked up to her. But she leapt forward, tore away his whip, and attacked again. Van Amburg rolled to the ground and, while the tigress tore at his chest with her claws, he seized her neck to keep her fangs at a distance. It was a terrible fight. The circus employees, stupefied at first, passively watched the horrible duel. One of them at last had the presence of mind to pass a knife to van Amburg through the bars of the cage. The tamer managed to stab

IMP. PAUL DUPONT 4, RUE DU BOULOI, PARIS · ATELIER PAL.

Tinsel . . .   Edith, but he died of tetanus a few days later.

The circus legend

The circus is richer than any other show in romantic stories, miserable or tragic ends, and these gradually have formed a legend. The life of van Amburg, which ended at the age of thirty-five in the circumstances related above, is a good example. As an adolescent he had tamed a bear in his native Kentucky. But this did not lead to the triumphs of the ring, for the bear overturned some beehives, and the neighbours complained. The young man told them to go and complain to the animal concerned, which they did, firing several bullets into his head. Maddened with rage, van Amburg attacked his bear's murderers and left them for dead. He had to take to the road. For four years he tramped round the world. But one fine day he came back to his native land for, just as in a novel, those he had left for dead had survived. But van Amburg returned only to leave once more. In the course of his travels, he met up with the Titus Menagerie. At this time (around 1830) the first animal-tamers were only just beginning to appear. The animals were controlled by whipping, which was one way of making them vicious. This had happened to Norah, a lioness in the Titus Menagerie. Norah already had wounded several employees when van Amburg detected from certain signs that the animal was not aggressive by nature, but had been spoiled by being badly treated. He declared that at the end of a month he would sleep with his head on her back. And he succeeded, to the great satisfaction of the owner

84

LE CHARMEUR DE SERPENTS

IMP. E. LÉVY, 13, RUE DE LA JUSSIENNE, PARIS.

of the menagerie, for at that time lion-tamers were hard to find.

But tragic or bizarre deaths are not unique to the lion-tamers. Andrew Ducrow, the athletic horseman whose poses drawing professors sent their students to admire, died insane after Astley's Amphitheatre in London burned down. The clown Boswell collapsed in the ring during an act. Another died from being kicked by a horse during a pantomime.

Naturally the collective imagination embroiders all this so that in the history of the circus it is even more difficult than elsewhere to disentangle facts from legends. There are at least three versions of the spectacular death of the clown Boswell as he hung upside down on the upright of a ladder. The most sensible may be that he died of a congestion of the brain brought on by the daily repetition of this exercise. The bizarre beliefs inspired by the circus are endless. For example, to explain the ascendancy of the trainers over the wild animals, two opposing explanations have been put forward, the one as false as the other. The first, dull and prosaic, maintains that the animals are doped, which would be more likely to leave the animals too stupefied to perform. The second, more mystical explanation, is that the trainer overpowers the animals through the fascination of his eyes. Unfortunately, animals do not allow themselves to be fascinated for the excellent reason that they tend to turn away their eyes as soon as they are stared at too fixedly. But these are harmless legends compared to the belief that was widespread in the nineteenth century, which maintained that the "monsters" shown in the ring were deliberately "fabri-

. . . and the exotic.

AU CIRQUE D'HIVER

1-5. Les chiens savants. — 6. Danseuse égyptienne. — 7. Mort de Cléopâtre. — 8. Antoine. — 9. Pantomime anglaise. — 10. Départ de Cléopâtre et d'Antoine.

cated" by the circus people who deformed children at birth.

George Washington's nurse

The genius of Phineas Taylor Barnum consisted of exploiting man's need for the marvellous into what ultimately became known as "The Greatest Show on Earth." He was an exploiter of a skill and scope that made him an outstanding character in the history of show business, and even in history itself, for his widespread activity made him a public figure. His career as an entrepreneur began in 1835 when he met in Tennessee a very old black woman named Joice Heth, whom he bought from a planter who had no doubt lost hope of making anything out of her. This is how Barnum described her in his memoirs: "She looked as if she might have been far older than her advertised age [161]. She was apparently in good health and spirits, but from age or disease, or both, was unable to change her position; she could move one arm at will, but her lower limbs could not be straightened; her left arm lay across her breast, and she could not remove it; the fingers of her left hand were drawn down so as nearly to close it, and were fixed; the nails on that hand were almost four inches long, and extended above her wrist; the nails on her two large toes had grown to the thickness of a quarter of an inch; her head was covered with a thick bush of grey hair; but she was toothless and totally blind, and her eyes had sunk so deeply in the sockets as to have disappeared altogether."

Barnum left Tennessee with his find and, one fine morning, the people of New York learned that they had in their city a relic whom up to that day they had scandalously left in oblivion: George Washington's nurse. Here, as a handbill distributed by Barnum announced, was the woman who "had had the signal honour of being the first to swaddle the weak infant who was destined in the future to lead our heroic ancestors to glory, to victory and to liberty."

There was a rush to Niblo's Garden where Barnum had Joice Heth on display. The Press talked of nothing else, and the public had their money's worth. Joice Heth sang hymns, songs of the War of Independence, and told a host of anecdotes about that glorious era. Barnum had taught her well. A European traveller who conducted a personal inquiry into this affair claimed that after the purchase, the showman had had the following dialogue with Joice Heth:

"So, my good woman, it was you who had the signal honour of nursing George Washington?"

"Oh no, good master! I just knew him when I was young. I spoke to him several times, that's all."

"But yes, yes, you're mistaken. You yourself nursed him with your milk. I'm sure of it, someone told me so."

Barnum took his find round all the towns of the United States. Then he sent her back to the country. She died there. An autopsy was carried out: some experts claimed that

Joice Heth was aged eighty at the very most. There were some journalists ill disposed enough to believe it. But others reassured the public by producing documents. People no longer spoke of Joice Heth. But they still talked about Barnum: it would need a whole book to describe all the fantastic phenomena he presented in the course of his career, ranging in size from the miniature General Tom Thumb, who was seen by an estimated twenty million spectators, to the gigantic twelve-foot-tall, six-and-a-half-ton elephant Jumbo.

Elephants at the plough

How could the public have fallen into the trap of these hoaxes, which their author himself described as "gigantic shams"? Historic certificates and pseudo-expertise alone were certainly not enough to carry conviction. In reality, this phenomenon is based on psychological and social truths. First there is the

The boxing kangaroo drawn by Albert Guillaume. (Bibliothèque Nationale, Paris)

principle pronounced by Phineas T. Barnum himself about people wanting to be made to believe things they know are not true. But it would be a mistake to believe that just any hoax would succeed. A flair for invention is required. For Barnum did not cheat as did the mountebanks who made their "giants" wear built-up soles, he did not fabricate freaks, he found them, and embellished them with his imagination. He had the art of injecting an air of unreality into a realistic scenario, and of adapting it to the social context. He had a remarkable feeling for crowd psychology and public relations, and in these fields he was unbeatable. In the Joice Heth affair, for example, he had struck the patriotic chord as well as the desire for the marvellous: each detail of his scenario was taken

straight out of American mythology. In the same way, when he later launched Tom Thumb, the dwarf general, the real stroke of genius was in having him play Napoleon before an English audience who could still remember Waterloo.

Barnum, more than any nineteenth-century entrepreneur, understood the value of effective advertising. The "woolly horse" he presented to the public clad in a coat with strange hairs met with great success because Barnum presented it as a sensational capture of an explorer in whom the public was deeply interested. The other element of success where "phenomena" are concerned is that they must be talked about and Barnum made that inevitable. After all, it mattered little whether the public believed or not in Washington's "nurse." The important fact was that they stirred themselves to come and pay to see her. To get something talked about, of course, there is nothing more effective than the Press: behind every one of Barnum's successes was to be found a Press campaign, carefully maintained scandals and controversies, all the things which it is pointless to describe since they have now become commonplace. Barnum had a very personal feeling for publicity. On one occasion, for example, he wanted to bring to the public's attention the new city he was building at Bridgeport, Connecticut, and he thought of harnessing an elephant to the plough, right near the railway line. The travellers spread the news, and soon the whole Press was talking of the unusual

Miss Estella. (Bibliothèque Nationale, Paris)

Opposite above: the open-air circus. A German print of 1840 after The Marvellous History of the Circus *by Henri Thétard.*

Opposite below: Madame Saqui, the famous tightrope walker, in an engraving by Alais. (Bibliothèque Nationale, Paris)

1856

attracting publicity, he transformed the Swedish coloratura Jenny Lind from a merely outstanding singer into a world-famous and beloved star, known universally as "the Swedish nightingale." With equal success he united the upper half of a monkey and the lower half of a fish and displayed it as the Fiji Mermaid. And, with similar gusto, Barnum had Noah's Ark and the Circus Maximus reconstructed. One day he even ordered Christopher Columbus's bones by telegram.

The Greatest Show on Earth

Despite his numerous achievements, Barnum cannot be credited with inventing the modern circus. Instead it evolved from its remote beginnings in Rome, with a stop to pick up clowns from the *commedia dell'arte*, and reappeared in a more modern guise in Astley's Amphitheatre. Circuses began touring the young United States in the eighteenth century. A man named Ricketts organized a circus that was actually attended by George Washington (without Joice Heth). Ricketts was followed by the unfortunate van Amburg and, later, by others who developed the idea of a two-ring show under the big tent. It remained for James Bailey to devise the flamboyant three-ring circus in the 1860s.

But, despite such a parade of facts, it is the name of Barnum that is most closely associated with the circus, for it was he who took the travelling tent show and made it into "The Greatest Show on Earth." Indeed, a spectacle of that name, produced by Barnum, opened in Brooklyn in 1871. Ten years later Barnum and his most successful competitor, three-ring Bailey, merged their operations, and the most spectacular of all circuses began to tour the world.

Above: members of the travelling circus. (Bibliothèque Nationale, Paris)
Opposite above: Barnum and Bailey's circus.
Opposite below: the tightrope walker Blondin, who became famous by crossing Niagara Falls on a high wire. (Opéra Library, Paris)

draught animals that were to be used. But when the incident had raised enough interest, Barnum sent the following note to the newspapers: "An elephant costs from fifteen to twenty thousand dollars. It is of no practical use in agriculture, its food is shockingly expensive. It can never get really acclimatized here. So, in America, elephants are useful only to Barnum, for advertising."

Thanks to Barnum's genius for

The kind of show that emerged did not have much in common with the sights of Astley's in London. The new schedule called for two matinees and an evening performance—an audience of ten to fifteen thousand spectators a day. The form of the circus had to be modified and a large number of administrators was also required: a circus like "The Greatest Show" required the day-to-day labour of about a thousand people. Circuses adopted all the methods of a modern business enterprise: a preliminary survey of the market to assess the probable audiences and hence to decide on the length of stay; animals; the organization, within the circus, of a whole city where the artists had eating and sleeping accommodations, and all indispensable commodities.

IL FAUT VOIR

BLONDIN

LE HÉROS DU NIAGARA,

AU

CHAMP DE COURSES DE VINCENNES,

Plateau de Gravelle.

Les titres authentiques prouvant *l'identité* de **BLONDIN** sont déposés aux bureaux de l'*Agence des Théâtres*, 15 boulevart des Italiens, et du *Petit Journal*, 21, boulevart Montmartre, où l'on peut prendre d'avance des billets sans augmentation de prix.

GREAT SUCCESS.

—

Dimanche prochain

EXERCICES

MERVEILLEUX

La Corde soutenue par deux mâts de plus de **120** pieds anglais de hauteur mesure- en longueur, d'ancre à ancre, plus de **800** pieds.

SUCCÈS

EXTRAORDINAIRE

CONSTATÉ

PAR LA

Première Ascension

DIMANCHE 15 JUILLET 1866,

A **4** HEURES PRÉCISES:

Paris.—Imp. Dubois et Ed. Vert, rue N.-D. de-Nazareth, 29.

*Above: Thétard,
The Marvellous
History of the Circus.
Below: General Tom
Thumb.
Opposite above:
Siamese twins.
Below: a Barnum
and Bailey clown.*

Of course, this huge scale had direct results on the very conception of the show. To fill the considerable space provided by the new rings, and to enable every spectator, wherever he was sitting, to see the show from a reasonable distance, they had to put on synchronized acts in three separate places. An arguable method, said one witness, for, carried away by curiosity, one tried to see everything, and saw everything badly. But the material conditions made it necessary. Huge efforts had to be made. The circuses run on this scale vied with each other as to which would show the greatest number of elephants or lions. They no longer featured any but stars with worldwide reputations. They put on grandiose pantomimes that were in part historical presentations such as *Nero*, or *The Queen of Sheba*, which "The Greatest Show" performed when it went to Paris in 1900. In short, a wide-screen Technicolor, super-spectacular before there was a Hollywood.

The death of the clowns

In a recent interview on French television, Emilien Bouglione declared, "Television is not destroying the circus, it is enabling the public to get to know it." It does that, certainly, but does it induce people to go there? That is debatable.

Circuses are disappearing. Clowns are changing again. One, who was on the same television programme as Bouglione was asked if children's reactions had changed and replied, "It's more difficult to make them laugh because they've seen a lot of things on television."

Everyone is aware of the changes television has wrought. But the decline of the circus must not be confused with that of the popular festivals, which was discussed earlier. For the circus, at least as it was conceived by Barnum and his associates, was on the threshold of our world: it was a show for the masses, utilizing all the resources of the exotic, of the sensational, of suspense, and of publicity. It is scarcely an exaggeration to say that the circus was the television of the nineteenth century. As it got under way at a time when traditional festivals were already declining, it served as a transition. It appears now to have been beaten on its own ground by other kinds of shows, which are far richer in suspense and in the exotic.

CHAPTER 7

HORSE RACING

If festivals are now in what may be considered a decline, popular shows still occupy an important place in our leisure time. Among the new forms of entertainment that are tending to replace the old ones—the circus, music hall, and even the cinema—two deserve special attention: horse racing and television games. This is because of their large audiences, and because they unite game and spectacle on a massive scale according to new principles.

The heroic era of horse racing began around 1600 when James I of England sketched out a racetrack at Newmarket. The first regular meetings were held there beginning in 1680. By 1780 the twelfth Earl of Derby had initiated the first sweepstake in horse-racing history, and the Epsom, or English, Derby is still a great event in race-enthusiasts' lives. England is also the cradle of the thoroughbred, the product of crossbreeding English and Arabian horses, whose descendants were entered into the Stud Book as early as 1700. Other important English innovations included the introduction of the steeplechase—an obstacle course that tested horses and their riders—which is still best known through the annual Grand National Steeplechase at Aintree, Liverpool. A Frenchman, however, was the inventor of the popular parimutuel system of betting, which was intro-

duced in the nineteenth century to reform gambling at the tracks.

The history of racing abounds in thrilling duels that have pushed the spectators' emotions to the limits of the bearable. To feel its delights, it is enough to have bet in a Grand Prix de Paris, which has remained famous, on Clairvoyant or Donatello II. The latter horse arrived in Paris with all the prestige bestowed on him by his breeder, Federico Tesio, who raced only first-rate horses in France. Clairvoyant was sired by Mon Talisman, who had been beaten ten years earlier in the same race by another Italian horse, Piterari. The race thus took on the semblance of a return match and was impatiently awaited by crowds of spectators. Clairvoyant, ridden by jockey Semblat, took the inside and was soon way out in front. The crowd waited for his adversary to attack. But, a hundred yards after the entry to the straight, at the end of the course, he had still not reacted. It is at this kind of moment that the spectator's anguish turns into incredulous stupor: what could be happening? Something very simple: following a common technique, a knot of horses was forming a blanket in front of the Italian horse to prevent him from showing his paces. But when all seemed lost, he succeeded in getting through. He then went at the post at a speed that had apparently never

Opposite: a race at Enghein.

been seen in living memory. He literally swallowed up the space separating him from his adversary. It was then Clairvoyant's backers who began to tremble, for his jockey had not seen Donatello break away, and was not trying to keep his lead by forcing the pace. His rival suddenly passed him like a whirlwind . . . but a few yards past the finish line. A great cry of relief and joy went up from the stands at the same time: Clairvoyant had escaped, and so had the spectators.

Finishes like this, which bring feelings to their height, are not exceptional. In 1939, in the same Grand Prix, when Pharis was three hundred yards from the post, he was still shut in and jostled by the crowd of horses. His jockey made the heroic decision to drop his horse back and take him to the outside. He started him running again, and in less than three hundred yards caught up with, and passed Tricameron, which had been running a long way in front. These feverish moments give the event a unique intensity and beauty. They help to make the racecourse a place haunted by passions not found in other stadia.

The living and the dead

The technicalities of laying, or placing, bets vary from one country to another, and even from one race to another. All we can give here is the bare bones of the matter, the respective positions of the participants: the state, the bookmakers, the owners, and the backers.

The state always wins. It levies about twenty per cent on all bets. This tapping seems to be a benevolent tax paid by all gamblers, a phenomenon whose social effects we will consider later. The bookmaker, too, is on the right side of the barrier: he

arranges things so as to limit the risks involved for him. As for the owner's gains, these are made up from the prizes he receives if his horses win, and, occasionally, by the advantageous bets he makes on his own horses when, sure of their form, he succeeds in betting on them without attracting the attention of other betters. The owner's chances of winning depend on the foresight of his trainer, and on the capital invested. The cost of buying a good racehorse and raising it is enormous, and frequent wins are necessary to pay it off. Ideally, therefore, one must own a lot of horses, and good ones.

The gamblers are, financially speaking, the victims since it is from them that all the people mentioned above get their profits. It remains to be seen if individually, setting aside the pleasure it gives them, they can break even in the long run. All the books on this subject include a chapter on "Can one win at horse racing?" The reader is referred to this fascinating heading to see how the question is answered in detail. The following are the minimum conditions to be met.

First, the true chances, or odds, of the horse on which you are to bet must be determined from several factors: the distance of the race, the condition of the track, the weights of the jockeys, the season (beware of mares in their season) and the horse's winning record. After fully weighing all these factors, and some others as well, do not forget to look at the horse's eyes and stomach before the race. If the eyes are dull, the horse appears fat, its coat is shiny or its forelegs are bandaged do not bet on it, even if all other factors are in its favour.

Granted the horse can win, there is still something more to be decided:

Above: the Queen arrives at Ascot on Gold Cup day.

Below: the public enclosures and fair at Epsom.

whether it is racing to win. To know that, you must know the trainer's plans. . . . If a week later, with the same horse, he can win a race that will bring ten times as much prize money, he may prefer to work him slowly instead of racing him today.

Once these problems are correctly resolved, you will know which are the "living" and which the "dead" in the race, that is, which do or do not have some chance of winning.

Of say, fourteen runners, there are usually hardly more than seven or eight "living": your chances are good if, added to a perfect comprehension of horses and men, you have a rudimentary knowledge of mathematics!

An awkward horse

It is not enough for your horse to win, it must also be profitable. The odds—that is the relationship between the amount staked and the amount won—must be taken into account when the better makes his choice. The odds depend on the horse's supposed chances as synthesized from the sum of the bets made on it. Obviously, if everyone bets on the same horse, if it wins it will only bring in a very small percentage to each better. That is why, when an owner wants to bet heavily on one of his horses of whose chances he is certain, and which has escaped the notice of other betters, he waits until the last minute so as not to bring down the odds and thus reduce his profits.

As a result, if a horse outclasses its competitors by so much that victory seems almost assured, it becomes practically impossible to bet on it. This happened in England in about 1770 with Eclipse. He never lost a race. He literally left his rivals standing so that one day his owner wagered in the following terms:

The racecourse.

"Eclipse first, the rest nowhere." And, in fact, they were several hundred yards behind when Eclipse passed the post. After some ten races he hardly returned one pound on a hundred, which made the profit when he won worthless unless very large sums were bet, a risk that small backers could not take, for there was always the possibility of an accident. Consequently, they were practically banished from the course. This virtual prohibition, which affected the majority of racegoers and added to the dissatisfaction of other owners, provoked violent reactions. Eclipse's owner received threatening letters. As his horse continued to win, the threats continued to pour in, and there were fears that the horse would be poisoned. Sullivan, who had raised and trained Eclipse became his horse's shadow. He tasted his food first, at the risk of being poisoned, went everywhere with him, and slept in his box. It must be said that this kind of precaution does not always succeed. It naturally excludes complicity on the part of the stable boys. One owner who had taken the same precautions saw his horse collapse one day in the middle of a race, apparently poisoned. Someone had managed to poison the horse somehow between the time he was taken from his stall and the time he reached the starting gate, although the owner had hardly let the horse out of his sight. For Eclipse the precautions proved effective since after a few months it was decided he would be more valuable as a stud than as a racer.

The stars and their shadows

Today all the men with some kind of power on the racetrack are more or less stars—especially the jockeys.

Earlier they were treated like coachmen, and had a hard life. In the morning they were made to swallow a violent purgative, then they walked some ten miles, and afterwards stood in front of a fire, not to warm up, but to "eliminate." The rest of the day was in keeping with this gruesome beginning. To-day steam baths have replaced all that. But jockeys still have a hard life: they must resolve the famous problem of weight by daily sacrifices. And there is the public's severity, its ignorance, and its rancour. How many times jockeys are unjustly accused of holding back a horse to let a crony win, or of "giving a bad ride." True, they are also credited with a power and skill that they do not possess. It is commonly believed that they know the secrets of the gods, that is that they know in advance which horse is going to win. Of course, the jockey's role is to think through the race while more or less keeping to the trainer's instructions. He also knows great and lesser secrets of which the public may not be aware, such as, for example, the existence of a weaker stable companion that is to be sacrificed, leading from the start of the race at a fantastic speed so as to exhaust the

Sea Bird.

Before the race.

other horses. But, despite what he knows, there is much that the jockey does not know: if not his rivals' manoeuvres, which he can anticipate, at least the exact abilities of the horses they are riding and the failings of his own horse. One day a horse caught up with three others that had taken the lead. Against all expectation, the horse stayed just behind them. His jockey could do nothing: they were three mares, and, recovering his chivalrous instincts— which are rarely encountered on racetracks—the stallion refused to make an effort that would have cost him nothing. In the end, in many cases, the jockey knows hardly any more than an informed racegoer. But then, one only gives credit to the rich, and that goes for magic powers as well.

Bookmakers, on the other hand, are the unofficial lords of the racetrack. In England they do not have the privilege of mystery. They operate legally and they have their own establishments. They are even becoming more numerous. The same does not apply to France and the United States where their activities are illegal. However, they exist. In France they are extremely discreet and their operations are modest. But in the United States their operations have for many years been big business, as the figures show. Films and novels have popularized the frightening figure of the bookie, and, while dramatizing him, have credited him with conduct more or less removed from reality; when he is not simply corrupt, the bookie appears as implacable. Pressuring, using blackmail, he pushes his unhappy clients to suicide or to committing murder to recover his money. On this particular point the legend is grossly exaggerated. A gambler is afraid above all of no longer being able to bet, and, as we saw in the story of Eclipse, a ban is for him the worst thing of all. The pressures the bookmaker can bring to bear on him by raising this threat are usually only effective enough to bring him to his senses.

On the other hand, the relationships of the bookies to the racing circle, often brought out in films, are very realistic. Their operations being illegal they would often meet serious trouble if they did not have with them—in some sort of association—people from racing circles who give them some protection. This protection is not, however, sufficient; they also need to "purchase" that of the local authorities. All this is expensive and cuts down their profits, which are, however, considerable. The profession does not seem to be on the verge of dying of lack of resources.

The tiercé

The *tiercé* in France and in Italy the *totocalcio* offer an extremely popular form of gambling, and a very successful one, as the figures show. Five million Frenchmen bet on the *tiercé* every Sunday. It consists of picking the three first horses of a race. The *tiercé* is not favoured by the knowledgeable because it leaves too large a part to chance. In a race with twenty-five horses there are 13,800 possible combinations. How under these conditions can one make a rational choice, given all the

Freddy Head and Yves Saint-Martin at Saint-Cloud.

imponderables that govern a horse's success? We should add that competing in the race chosen for the *tiercé* there are sometimes novices that are almost unknown to the public. In short, the knowledgeable accuse the *tiercé* of being a lottery, not a game controlled by the rules of the turf.

This, however, is precisely why it has been so successful. The basic principle of the *tiercé* is that by

Lester Piggott.

merely placing a small bet of three francs one can win very large sums, especially if none of the favourites is placed. It is not uncommon for the winners in this system to collect ten thousand francs for a stake of one franc (about twenty United States cents or seven pence). This is easily explained: the sum of the stakes to be shared among the winners, after deducting for the percentage levied by the state and the racing societies, amounted in the 1971 Prix Narquois to 73,829,847 francs. The chances of winning are, of course, slim. But psychologically that is secondary since the essential factor is the hope of a worthwhile win, and especially that in losing one cannot lose too much. This concept has put betting in everyone's reach; it has democratized it. There is no need to be acquainted with the gambler's excitement to take big risks, it is enough to queue up at the *tiercé* office. Betting is no longer an aristocrat's luxury, one can taste its joys and avoid its terrors. With the *tiercé*, there is no danger of ruining one's family. Betting is no longer, as formerly, a fault and a vice. It is a healthy amusement that is made comfortable by the absence of risks and that enlivens the weekend.

Who is it who dreams of winning a miraculous fortune? Generally, and understandably, it is the less fortunate. Eighty-five per cent of the people who bet on the *tiercé* stake no more than three francs, although some combinations that cost very little more offer a much higher chance of winning. The *tiercé* is a social phenomenon: it gives the participant the hope of escaping from his hard life, it introduces into his life where the chips are already down the new dimension of luck and the opportunity of dreaming of a future offering room to fantasy and the unexpected.

Left: the Start of the Paris Grand
Steeplechase, 20th June 1971.
Above: jockeys at Enghein racecourse.
Below: the Finish.

An illusion? Some *tiercistes* take a very wise view of things, like the man who, having won twice in eight years, betting regularly, calculated that he could thereafter continue to bet in the same way until he reached the age of seventy-seven without spending a penny other than his winnings. Of course, one can look at the *tiercé* from this angle, that is as a pleasure that if the worst comes to the worst will not cost very much. But the repeated disappointments breed in some people a real frustration, which is expressed in obsessive attempts to cheat, also, not always in the most intelligent way.

In fact the most serious criticisms that have been levelled at the *tiercé* concern economic and social factors —that is that the state, under a cloak of democracy, collects a part of the stakes, and is thus levying an extra tax on the income of the people who can least afford it.

Totocalcio

This formula by which gambling is grafted on to a spectacle is characteristic of our civilization. Long before the *tiercé* started in France in 1954, a weekly competition forecasting the results of football matches had spread from one end of Europe to another. In these pools one has to decide the results of thirteen matches (draw, home or away win) that are listed on the coupon. This game, already current in Switzerland and England in the 1930s, developed greatly after World

War II, especially in Italy where in 1970 the *totocalcio* handled sums amounting to 7,400,000,000 lire. The *totocalcio* even attracts foreigners, who have their coupons sent in by intermediaries who travel between one country and the other. The *totocalcio*'s success is based on the same principle as that behind the *tiercé*: the possibility of large gains for a stake of a few pennies. (France has not yet adopted this form of betting because there would be too great a risk of competition with the *tiercé*, whose role it would be duplicating.)

The economic and social effects of these games are considerable. As in the *tiercé*, only a part of the amounts collected are redistributed to the winners. The rest goes to the state or into the coffers of sporting associations. In this way they provided funds for a large programme of swimming-pool building in some parts of Germany, and in Italy the installations for the 1960 Rome Olympics were financed in this way. The direct consequence is that the state is relieved of costly building programmes.

The *totocalcio* is, therefore, a real financial enterprise. Perhaps the game finds an advantage in it: in Sweden recently a man won a fortune by filling in his coupon according to the instructions of his little girl whom he had asked to toss a die thirteen times. But the entertainment? Inevitably, it is becoming commercialized, with all that that implies for the sport. Now only the result counts, the entertainment is becoming less and less pure. It might even disappear entirely behind the figures and abstractions the gambler manipulates, if television was not there to reinstate it visually into its world, as it does for football matches. The same is true for horse racing in Britain where meetings are extensively covered by television. Thus, in this way, the gambler, who has once more become a spectator, can rediscover, if not the true atmosphere of the racetrack, at least the feelings of the racegoer in the grandstands.

For genuine enthusiasts, however, nothing compares with really being at the track. Witness, for example, the immense crowds that swarm to Lexington each spring for America's most popular race, the Kentucky Derby. Thousands and thousands of people flock to the Derby, bringing box lunches to the infield of the track when the stands are so full that no one can move. The less fortunate, crowded in the infield, are so tightly packed in that they cannot even get to a booth to make a bet. Yet they come—it is for these devoted fans a festival with a carnival atmosphere, a ritual to be repeated annually for the almost inexplicable pleasure of being where the action is, rather than in front of a television thousands of miles from the event.

An episode from Interneige 65.

CHAPTER 8

TELEVISION GAMES

Now that we are well beyond the middle of the twentieth century, we might ask where are the clowns and mountebanks of modern times. We do not have far to look to find the answer. They are on the lighted box in the corner of the room, telling jokes of every vintage and various degrees of distinction, acting in plays, performing in compressed circuses, and selling merchandise that will cure everything from fallen arches to leaky roofs. The wonder of it is that we need not leave the house to have these marvels at our immediate disposal.

This home-style combination of festival and spectacle reaches its peak in television games. In this remarkable, updated version of yesterday's diversions, the person sitting in front of the television is both spectator and player. He is a spectator, since in principle, at least, he is not directly concerned; he is the incarnation of the "innocent bystander," who can participate or not as he chooses. If the game interests him, the spectator lives each moment as if he were the participant he sees on the screen. And, in some kinds of television games, he may, unlike our innocent bystander, participate by picking up his telephone to assist one of the contestants.

Being given the choice of participating or just watching the spectacle may be one of the reasons why television games have achieved such widespread popularity. Indeed, at different times and at different places, these games have affected the daily life of entire nations. In Italy, not too long ago, the streets emptied during the showing of *Campanile Sera*. About a decade and a half ago, Americans seemed universally to be glued to the weekly performance of "The 64,000 Dollar Question."

In the beginning was the marvellous lighted box. Immediately came the problem of what to put on the box that would have the widest possible appeal. The resulting schedules, according to most interested and totally partial observers, have been dramatically mediocre. For every hour of *The Forsyte Saga*, there were at least one hundred hours of soap operas. For every minute of symphony concert there were fifty hours of rag-tag vaudeville only slightly resuscitated from its last appearance in the provinces. And last, but far from least, for every hour of intellectual conversation, there have been two thousand hours of games, ranging in challenge from the mildly thought-provoking quiz programme to total audience participation in the pursuit of truth or the consequences of falsehood. But then, there are all those hours to fill and all those millions of people to divert.

The dinner dishes are put away

and the family is reunited. The home lights dim. The box light blooms. A man sits in an "isolation booth" pensively sucking his lower lip. He is alone with his brain, which must from some grey recess produce the right answer to questions about the Roman emperors. The audience in the studio and at home is hushed, tense, breathless. The master of ceremonies reads from his little white card, "What was the name of Caligula's horse?" Silence. Beads of sweat break out on a thousand brows.

The MC, at last acknowledging the too-long time lapse, proclaims in tones of one-hundred-per-cent treacle, "I'm sooo sorry Mr Sweeney. It was Incitatus." Next contestant. . . .

Or, better yet, next question, which should be: "Why Caligula's horse?" "Did he have only one?" Of course not, he had hundreds; but as you surely recall he treated Incitatus as an idol. The horse's very slumbers were watched over by slaves. The important question— and the one that could not be asked —is why did the Roman citizens permit Caligula this extravaganza with a horse? Since the answer would require more than a simple phrase, it has no place in the world of the quiz show. Yet, intellectually, it is the only interesting question. If it is not put, the viewers' brains will be filled with only a few disconnected facts. And this is the reverse of what culture, or the understanding of the reasons behind things, should be. It should be emphasized that we do not deny the value, still less the cultural impact of television, nor do we wish indiscriminately to contrast it with books, music, and museums as is so often done—but we must recognize that culture can find a place on television only when it abandons

random dips into the encyclopedias for the *hors d'œuvres* of knowledge.

Farce

Somewhere in the great void beyond the quiz shows, which reveal to us the little-known secret illnesses of kings and the peculiar habits of small mammals, there is broad farce.

When farces were performed in a theatre, the comedy took place in a completely fictitious world, a world ruled by conventions. In this farcical kind of television game, the reverse is attempted: comic conventions are given the appearance of being true to life, spontaneous, authentic. But everywhere the spectator can see the strings: he is, finally, neither at the theatre, nor enjoying the broad humour of "life." This false spontaneity fails because in this sphere, one must cheat thoroughly, or not at all.

The virtues of the close-up

Some question-masters, aware of the pitfalls we have just discussed, and more particularly of the monotony engendered by the mechanical display of a knowledge culled from encyclopedias, attempt to give television games a human content. The first step is the judicious selection of the questions to be answered by the contestant. The trick is to avoid facts, dates and, generally, everything that could not strike any chord in the viewer. In these game shows there are anecdotes, picturesque or lively details, substantiated by illustrations on film, sketches, or documents. These illustrations cannot be too long or the reporting smothers the game. According to the specialists, two minutes is the maximum, so that the questioning can be kept up at a fairly rapid pace.

Feats of skill . . .

In fact, their role is only to awaken the viewers' curiosity and make them even more receptive to the drama unfolding before them. For the television game—this may be the explanation of its success—is a drama that affords a special intoxicating pleasure. This pleasure, composed of excitement, anguish, and relief, is felt by any player. But in this case, it takes on a special form: ordinary players do not observe themselves, and if they observe their adversaries, it is in an attempt to get some information, not for the pleasure of watching on their faces the pangs of indecision. In television games, on the other hand, every second of the drama can be followed, thanks to the close-ups transmitted by the camera. In these the slightest shadow, the slightest gleam on the face or in the eyes of the man in front of us becomes meaningful.

Popular stars

. . . and serious competition and farce. (Interneige *and* Intervilles)

If the contestant's reactions do indeed have so much emotional power over us, it is naturally because we are identifying with him. One can sometimes see on the faces of the audience at television games the same tension, the same anguish as on the face of the contestant. But this identification is not automatic, we are not interested in just anybody, which is why the choice of contestants in television games is of so much importance.

The contestants are not chosen simply for their abilities. The "good contestant" is not only a knowledgeable person, but also one who can inspire people's liking. The interest the audience shows in him depends on human factors and on his televised presence, which is the unknown quantity the producer must detect. It is, of course, immensely difficult to assess this quality in advance. A contestant who, at rehearsals, seems to have the required qualities may appear cold or neutral in front of the camera, lacking the human warmth that attracts liking. And, without liking, there can be no identification. The viewer wants to recognize in the contestant a happy and improved image of himself.

In other words, the way a contestant answers the questions put to

him, his reactions, his comments, are of more importance to the game than the content of his answers. The contestant who is quick and witty is a winner in more ways than one, for curtness and solemnity breed boredom and apathy in the audience. The importance of the human factor has led some producers to look for contestants whose lives or personal idiosyncrasies will at once create this indispensable positive feeling. In this way some programmes have featured unique personalities such as the blind man questioned on the Bible, or the shoemaker who knew all about opera.

In the final analysis, the public wants nothing less than a contestant with the unknown quality that makes him a star. For in the public's eyes the contestant who is out of the ordinary is a star: he is even the superlative example of the popular star. Pop-singers and film-stars, however simple they may be, always give the impression of belonging to a different world. But the star of a television game belongs to the commonplace, he is a part of everyone's daily life. The viewer does not

*Just like school . . .
"The Last of the
Five" with Pierre
Tchernia.*

and losing are then the sole elements of suspense. This is particularly true in the United States where contestants may win thousands of dollars if they perform well—that is, answer all the questions correctly —on a game show. In the triumph of the Right Answer, however, lie the seeds of severe boredom—a fact that led more than one producer in the past not only to coach his players on gestures and grimaces but also on how to reply to questions as well. The resulting scandals dimmed the public hunger for these spectacles for only a short time, however, and the quiz game seems to have carved a secure niche in the daily TV schedule. One can only marvel that there are so many quick-witted people available to take their places behind the gaming table week after week and month after month.

Television in general, and the game shows in particular, provide a continuous and rather saddening contrast to the wonder of past festivals and spectacles. The man of leisure who works only forty or so hours a week, has over 120 hours of time left to fill. One outdoor performance of the *commedia dell'arte*, an annual Feast of Fools, a spectacular combat between a trainer and his lions under a tent fifty miles from his home, are scarcely enough to fill the time. And television does do that. In so doing, it has borrowed and reformed every type of entertainment that has ever been created. We easily discovered the new home of the clowns and the mountebanks that we sought at the beginning of the chapter, but it is not certain that we have found the joyous spontaneity of their spectacles in the neatly framed and carefully orchestrated television games and diversions that have reshaped man's leisure hours today.

feel alienated from him. The game-star's adventure could be his own, if he wanted. He sees in the star a successful version of Mr Everybody, a mythical figure: hence the flood of letters and protests aimed at the producer when a well-liked contestant loses a game.

Behind the scenes

It is a temptation, especially in the countries where the competition between several commercial channels leads to a continuous search for the sensational, to fabricate the stars the public admires, who keep them silent and attentive in front of their television sets. But the sensational at any price leads to trickery. Here we touch on that most fundamental problem—money.

Loss or gain is in television games the essential element of the excitement. The psychological effectiveness of "double or nothing" needs no further demonstration. Winning

Televised games in France.

CHAPTER 9

PERSPECTIVES

There may seem to be a virtually unbridgeable gap between the Roman spectators packed into the Colosseum thirsting for blood and even the most impassioned spectator sitting in front of his television set rooting for the contestant in a quiz game. Given a choice between the thirst for blood and the thirst for even the tiniest scrap of knowledge, we should surely choose the latter and congratulate ourselves on the splendid upward march of mankind.

Alas for the great-staircase-of-history theory, the change has been in spectacle names rather than spectacle types. Indeed, the great staircase of history becomes more like a stepping-stone to reality when one recalls that during a recent presidential campaign in the United States, the victors of baseball's World Series had a bigger reception in their hometown than did the president, who foolishly chose the same day to visit that community.

And, one must ask, how much difference is there between the Romans, who urged their gladiators on to bigger and better deeds of valour, and the millions of Americans who suffer what seems to be a temporary loss of sanity each Saturday and Sunday during the football season when they gather in stadiums all over the land to shout, sing, sigh, and shove in their excitement over the behaviour of the well-armoured

men on the field of combat? The same kind of nearly delirious vacation from reality can be seen, of course, at any soccer match in Europe or South America. One must ask, too, how much difference there really is between the triumphs of adoration enjoyed by a Cruyff and by his forerunners in Rome. The same is true, as well, of bullfighting, horse racing, cricket, and even so decorous a sport as tennis, where the audience may confine itself to whispers of encouragement, while surging inwardly with the passion of a gladiatorial fan.

As a first conclusion, we may feel quite safe, therefore, in assuring ourselves that spectacles of one sort or another seem to be here to stay. But what of the fantastic festivals of yesteryear? A Feast of Fools seems inconceivable in modern dress. The joyous Christmas of the illustrated nineteenth-century books is clearly becoming more commercialized each year. And even so simple a children's holiday as Hallowe'en becomes more and more a matter of going through the motions to the tinkling of candy- and card-manufacturers' cash registers. Perhaps with so many alternative methods of blowing off steam at our disposal, we no longer yearn for the annual explosion of festive gaiety. Besides one has the choice of so many other ways of entertaining

Opposite: Viareggio Carnival.

oneself—live and televised sports, movies, concerts, games, circuses, and yes, even a festival or two that have managed to survive in spite of the lure of other activities.

Pre-Lenten carnivals of some distinction and fervour are still held in Rio de Janeiro, Nice, Binche, and, of course, New Orleans. The carnival in New Orleans even boasts a certain originality, as it goes on for nearly two months and ends in the selection of a carnival king. For the man in the street, the New Orleans Mardi Gras festivities reach their peak in the procession of splendid floats that are representative of a theme that varies from year to year.

Above left: the Gilles of Binche Carnival. Below left: characters from the Malmedy Carnival (Belgium). They are holding the sticks with which they grab the spectators' arms and legs.

Above and right: carnival scenes in Germany.

Recently, for example, the procession included twenty-nine floats representing the works of the science-fiction writer Jules Verne. Mardi Gras in New Orleans embodies local traditions that are mainly more aristocratic than plebeian in origin. But, as we saw in the committee carnivals of the nineteenth century, each successive year sees the spirit of the event becoming more ritualized and less spontaneous. It almost seems now that the show is held more for tourists than for any other reason. The same thing is true, as well, of such popular carnivals as those at Nice and in Germany's Rhineland.

But what of the future? Aldous Huxley, among others, presented a rather alarming view of entertainment-to-be in *Brave New World* with its mixture of "soma" and movies, which are in fact a complete environment affecting all the senses by judicious dispensation of appropriate aromas and "feelies." With a visionary's omniscience, Huxley may not have missed the mark by too much. Consider, for example, the popularity of such total environment experiences as New York City's Electric Circus, a once popular discotheque with its blaze of light and music to which one "did one's own thing." In Paris, similarly, a Magic Circus was besieged by crowds eager for the atmosphere of avant-garde protocol and the rather extraordinary mixture of show and festival.

On still another level, such folk-rock festivals as the one at Woodstock show that even generations weaned on television have a taste for disguise (witness the number of "frontiersmen," "farmers," "Indians," and "pirates"!), playing games, and above all, a fervour to be rid of all restraint—parental, pedagogic, or even subliminal. The

first of these rock festivals, at any rate, did have about them something of the wild freedom that marked the Feast of Fools. But, and it may say a great deal about the disappearance of festivals in our time, as soon as the need became clear the entrepreneurs moved in and organized the freedom—a clear contradiction in itself.

A different, and perhaps even more prophetic, form of organization is evident in the two gigantic amusement parks run by the Disney Corporation in Anaheim, California, and Orlando, Florida. These lavish establishments offer literally everything a spectacle-lover or a festival-seeker could want, and one has the choice of staying for a day, a week, a month, or longer. Here truly is the total environment for diversion as you will see if you consider the resources offered at Disney World in Florida. On a forty-three-square-mile tract you will find Fantasyland, Main Street, USA, Tomorrowland, Adventureland, Frontierland, Liberty Square, and, as if that were not enough, there is a region called Fort Wilderness for campers, and every kind of sports facility, plus two resort hotels, one in Polynesian style, the other a model of modernity. One can tour virtually the entire area by monorail—a marvel of lightweight, streamlined, noiseless design that even glides through the contemporary resort and out again.

A glimpse inside any of the feature areas is an adventure for both spectacle- and festival-lovers. Fantasyland has an eighteen-story Cinderella's Castle, concerts by marching bands, parades of Disney characters like Mickey Mouse, and a ride on a submarine called appropriately "20,000 Leagues Under the Sea." For the nostalgic, Main Street, USA, offers the America of 1890 to

Above: some areas, such as the Tyrol, carefully preserve their traditions.

Below: carnival float in New Orleans.

1910, with horse-drawn vehicles, a Victorian park, and a magnificent railroad station. The opposite side of that coin is, naturally, Tomorrowland, with its twenty-story Space Mountain, where you can pilot your own space vehicle, or should you choose, a Grand Prix racecourse where you can compete in a more traditional automotive event. The United States' fast-vanishing Frontierland is recaptured in full sentimental trappings visible in part from a keel boat, a log raft, or a sternwheeler—take your choice. The thrill of a lion-trapper or an anthropologist is available in Adventureland where one can take a jungle cruise in ships with such evocative names as *Irrawaddy Irma*, or *Bomokandi Bertha*. Once aboard, a pith-helmeted guide points out the local fauna, including awesomely authentic-looking elephants, hippos, lions, and even headhunters, and helps calm one's almost real fears travelling through mysterious caves and across rushing rapids where, one is assured, braver men have perished.

This miracle of packaging, planning, and programming suggests that the festival-spectacle of tomorrow may well be such resorts where one can vacation without for a moment losing the spirit of holiday, as one might so easily do if one was

Above: the Grand Magic Circus

Opposite: Disneyland.

staying at a more ordinary establishment. The inevitable imitations of Disneyland and Disney World that will spring up may be more visibly plastic and unreal than these prototypes, partly because they will not be so close to the source of our own dreams of the past, manufactured as they were at the Disney studios in Hollywood. Nevertheless it seems almost inevitable that our future filled with ever-growing leisure hours will demand something along the lines of this total entertainment environment. The Romans had to leave the Colosseum to eat and sleep, their modern counterparts can literally camp amidst their diversions, waking each day to a new round of joyful diversion from reality—until the money runs out! And, during the long weeks of work, there is always television to stave off any sense of dullness and low spirits. In sum, we may have lost much of the spontaneity of old, but in a world faced by such dire threats as atomic extermination, overpopulation, and ecological disaster, we seem to be finding enough different ways of manufacturing spectacles to take our minds off these more profound issues for a few hours each day. Whether we are fiddling while our own Rome burns is a matter for philosophers to decide.

ACKNOWLEDGMENTS

Allardet: pp. 110, 114. Allemand: 14. Atlas-Photo-Berrier: 124. Atlas-Photo-Jouanne: 125. Atlas-Photo-Kerladec: 123. Atlas-Photo-Tondeur: 19. Belsan: 11. Bernard: 126. Bessé: 33. Bibliothèque Nationale, Paris: 42, 47, 48, 49, 50, 51, 74, 75, 78, 88, 90. Bibliothèque Royale de Bruxelles: 30. Blauel: 16, 17. Boudet-Lamotte: 13, 21, 22, 23, 25. Boutroux: 116. British Museum: 44. Cacco: 51, 65. C.G.T.: 120. C.G.T. Robelus: 120. Descamps: 115. Ellebé: 12. E.N.I.T.: 13, 63, 118. Flammarion: 26, 29, 32, 36, 38, 39, 42, 43, 45, 52, 53, 60, 61, 64, 65, 66, 68, 69, 71, 72, 75, 76, 78, 79, 80, 81, 83, 84, 85, 86, 87, 88, 89, 91, 92, 94, 97, 99, 100, 102, 105, 106, 107, 109. Giraudon: 12, 25, 29, 31, 46, 51, 55, 56, 59, 66, 67, 69. German Tourist Office: 121. Giraudon-Alinari: 11. Giraudon-Lauros: 10, 20, 34, 37, 40, 41. Hano: 44. Henry: 21. Japanese Tourist Office: 125. Landenszentrale für politische Bilding: 15, 19. Library of Paris: 115. Martin: 18. Marlin: 8, 113. ONAT: 59, 124. Pic: 46. Ricoupé: 98, 100, 101, 103, 104. USIS: 91, 93, 117, 127.

FURTHER READING

Bradbrook, M. C. *The Rise of the Common Player* London: Chatto and Windus 1962

Brody, A. *English Mummers and Their Plays* Philadelphia: University of Pennsylvania Press 1971. London: Routledge and Kegan Paul 1971

Chambers, R. Ed. *Book of Days* New York: Gale Research 1967

Ducharte, P. L. *The Italian Comedy* New York and London: Dover 1965 and 1968

Epsom, N. *Spanish Fiestas* London: Cassell 1968. New York: A. S. Barnes 1969

Fenner, M. S. *Circus, Lure and Legend* Eaglewood Cliffs, N.J.: Prentice-Hall 1970

Fitzsimmons, R. *Barnum in London* London: Bles 1969. New York: St Martin's Press 1970

Fowler, W. W. *Roman Festivals of the Period of the Republic* U.S.A. and London: Kennikat Press 1969 and 1970

Henry, M. *Gaudenzia, Prince of the Palio* Chicago: Rand McNally 1960. London: Wm Collins 1960

Henry, M. *King of the Wind* Chicago: Rand McNally 1948. London: Wm Collins 1948

Kuck, V. de *The Fun They Had* Cape Town: Howard Timmins 1955

McKetchnie, S. *Popular Entertainments Through the Ages* U.S.: Benjamin Bloom

McNiell, F. M. *The Silver Bough* Glasgow: McLellan 1961

May, E. C. *Circus From Rome to Ringling* New York and London: Dover 1932 and 1971

Miller, K. *Saint George: A Christmas Mummers Play* Boston: Houghton Mifflin 1967

Mincielli, R. L. *Harlequin* New York: Knopf 1968

Nicoll, A. *The Development of the Theatre* London: Harrap 1966. New York: Harcourt Brace Jovanovich 1967

—— *Masks, Mimes and Miracles* U.S.A.: Cooper Square Publications 1931

—— *The World of Harlequin* New York and London: Cambridge University Press 1963

Nye, R. *The Unembarrassed Muse: The Popular Arts in America* U.S.A.: Dial 1970

Priestley, *The Wonderful World of the Theatre* New York: Doubleday 1969

Strutt, J. *Sports and Pastimes of the People of England* Bath: Forecrest Publishing 1969

INDEX

Page numbers in italics indicate an illustration.